Mary, After the Queen

The Hewins family, 1915. Top row: George senior, Else, George junior. Middle row: Emma, with Mary on her knee, Ede, Jess. Front row: Cyril, Flo, Jim

Mary,
After the Queen

MEMORIES OF A WORKING GIRL

ANGELA HEWINS

With a Foreword by
PAUL THOMPSON

Oxford   New York
OXFORD UNIVERSITY PRESS
1985

Oxford University Press, Walton Street, Oxford OX2 6DP

London New York Toronto
Delhi Bombay Calcutta Madras Karachi
Kuala Lumpur Singapore Hong Kong Tokyo
Nairobi Dar es Salaam Cape Town
Melbourne Auckland
and associated companies in
Beirut Berlin Ibadan Mexico City Nicosia

Oxford is a trade mark of Oxford University Press

British Library Cataloguing in Publication Data

Hewins, Mary Elizabeth
Mary, after the Queen : memories of a working girl.
1. Stratford-upon-Avon (Warwickshire)—Social
life and customs 2. England—Social life and
customs—20th century
I. Title   II. Hewins, Angela
942.4'89   DA690.S92
ISBN 0–19–212242–8

Library of Congress Cataloging in Publication Data

Hewins, Mary.
Mary, after the Queen.
1. Hewins, Mary. 2. Stratford-upon-Avon
(Warwickshire)—Biography. 3. Hewins family.
I. Hewins, Angela II. Title.
DA690.S92H49 1985   942.4'8908   84–29630
ISBN 0–19–212242–8

Phototypeset by Wyvern Typesetting Ltd, Bristol
Printed in Great Britain by
St. Edmundsbury Press Ltd,
Bury St. Edmunds, Suffolk

FOR SIS
and Else and Ede and Jess and Kate
and all the others
who have gone

Acknowledgements

The assistance of West Midlands Arts is gratefully acknowledged. Most of the photographs in the text belong to the Hewins family. I should also like to thank warmly Vera Cooke (who carried the school photograph on page 12 in her handbag for over fifty years!), and Mary Halladay for the photograph on page 37. Photographs on pages 52, 114, and 117 are reproduced by kind permission of the Shakespeare Birthplace Trust.

The extract from 'The Song of Wandering Aengus' on page xvii is taken from *The Poems of W. B. Yeats*, edited by Richard J. Finneran (New York: Macmillan, 1983), and is reproduced by kind permission of Michael B. Yeats, Macmillan London Ltd, and Macmillan New York.

My gratitude extends also to Dorothy Eagle, whose advice and encouragement came just when I needed them, and to Mary and Brian, to whom my debt is inestimable.

Foreword
by Paul Thompson

Stratford-upon-Avon today exudes a scented, luxuriant past: from the theatre waterfront through to the ample trees around the stone-spiralled parish church, a sustained image of manicured half-timbering, well-kempt gardens and cream teas. It is as if the town wanted itself thought of as conceived immaculate, and handed down unimpaired through time, rather than as a place made, maintained and reshaped through human effort and pain. Shakespeare of course knew better. That is why, as you read, first in *The Dillen* and then *Mary, After the Queen*, the story of five generations of the Hewins family of Stratford, you have a sense of one of Shakespeare's subplots come alive: the heroes and heroines now the housewives and whores, craftsmen, labourers and gravediggers, whom before we had no more than fleetingly glimpsed. It feels like the rediscovery of a common heritage, a past lost, yet also fascinatingly familiar.

The thread which holds both books together is the life of George Hewins, born a hundred years ago. In *The Dillen* the voice is his, in *Mary* his daughter's; and the subtle differences in language and tone between the two are indications of the sensitivity and care with which both of their stories have been recorded and put together by Angela Hewins. With George, we are captured by the storyteller's image and turn of word; with Mary, much more by an open honesty. But they recognizedly belong to each other.

George begins his story among the rivermen at the wharf, Victorian Stratford's commercial underbelly. Born of a failed abortion and deserted by his mother as an infant, he was brought up by his great-aunt in her common lodging house, in the company of down-and-outs, casuals and prostitutes. Apprenticed to a local builder through her determination, he fell for early marriage and failed to serve his full time. Once married, as his children increased relentlessly his life became an unending struggle for work, turned to bitterness through his savage mutilation in the First World War.

Mary's memories begin after the war, when her crippled father was the Church School caretaker. 'I can't remember anything about school much, 'cept cleaning it.' Her world was the council estate and the new factories at the edge of the town, which the history-seekers pass, but fail to see, on their way in. She re-creates it vividly: on the one hand, the rows between her parents, and the appalling pain which both suffered from ill-health; on the other the loyalty which emerges, for example, when her sister is dying of tuberculosis, or in sometimes rougher ways when she gets into trouble herself. For Mary falls in turn, giving to old George his final role as doting grandfather of the next generation's orphan child. 'He lifted him so gently: like a chick . . . I thought: E thinks of the ole man as 'is Dad . . . They were inseparable. That did used to upset me, but there was nothing I could do about it.'

If a 'lovechild' to the family, the infant Hewins was made a good deal less welcome by the keeper of Stratford's conscience. 'Good news! There's a babby been born!', old George told the Vicar proudly. 'So I 'ear,' said the Vicar, 'and I wants it *out*, this day, this minute, Hewins! *And* er! Else your job goes, and the house!' Only the doctor's pleadings saved them.

George's best stories were woven around incidents, and other people. Mary can have a comparable pungency—I think of her comment on her deserting boyfriend, 'It was like trying to keep a fox'—but it is, above all, her insights into her own feelings that make her memories remarkable. She conveys in a tellingly simple way what it was to be an adolescent girl on a small-town council estate in the Thirties: the chaffing at the factory, the fun of dressing up and going out, the power of physical attraction, the agony of feeling her own body awkward. Still more unusual is her account of how she first rejected her own baby—'for days after he was born I hadn't wanted to look at him'—but eventually gave in to her mother's pressure to feed him, and was won to him. 'I didn't want to, I didn't want to love him. But as soon as he was there, at my breast, soon as I'd felt his little hands and his little mouth, I thought: E's mine! E's all mine!'

Love, pain, fun, death are the stuff of great drama just because they are also the common experience of ordinary lives. Once you have learnt to listen—whether, like Angela Hewins, as an oral historian; or as a therapist; or from sheer interest—you can find fascination in *any* person's life. But if the intrinsic interest is shared, the way of telling is not. *The Dillen* is a masterpiece of spoken autobiography because George Hewins had a rare gift for telling a story. The more straight-forward candour of *Mary, After the Queen* is in itself less unusual.

But the two books put together grow to become much more. The closest parallel is perhaps in the work of Oscar Lewis in Mexico, as in *The Children of Sanchez*. Just because *The Dillen* and *Mary* differ in perspective as well as in generation, and because one is by a man and the other is by a woman, they give us, for one English working-class family, a uniquely deep and intimate history.

Editor's Preface

Mary aged fourteen

This is the story of a working girl, the dreams she dreamt and the rivers she had to cross. A story close to my heart for many reasons, like *The Dillen* it is neither novel or biography, but a compilation of spoken memories, from the transcripts of tapes, and from notebooks. Nor is it a sequel to the first book, although the subjects are related. Called Mary 'after the Queen',* she was George Hewins's youngest child, the baby born as he went off to war: one of those ends that was also a beginning.

* *The Dillen*, edited by Angela Hewins (OUP, 1982), p. 133.

The circumstances of recording Mary's story were different. She was much younger and more mobile than George; we talked out of doors as well as in, and consequently a tape recorder and microphone were not always as practicable as they had been in the old man's cottage. George was a story-teller, in the ancient tradition; Mary, on the other hand, liked a 'good chat' with whoever happened to drop by. I realized early on that I would never have a monopoly on her attention. There was considerable social interaction during interviews or chats, sometimes vociferous, and drawing from communal, family memory, which had not been the case with *The Dillen*:

'Ey d'you remember our Else and the *violin recital*?'
Much laughter and badinage.

Sometimes, especially when later days were being recalled, another, younger voice intervened, adding *his* memories:

'That was the night the Americans came . . . You *must* remember . . . The noise of the horns . . .'
'The noise of the horns woke me!'

Like a whiff of scent in the air—lilac? lime trees?—that no one can quite put a name to, the resulting tale is dreamlike yet firmly bound to earth, innocent and coarse, figured and unfinished. Therein, for me, lies the beauty of spoken recollection. Also, because I cared for *The Dillen* too (a tale set in late Victorian and Edwardian England), there was the fascination of seeing familiar characters moving in a different drama, of hearing them speak with different tongues. Only the backcloth seemed the same: Stratford-upon-Avon. But even that, on closer examination, had changed.

Industrial development came late to some parts of Middle England. Not many years after the end of the First World War, when Mary's story begins, a report* was published by Stratford-upon-Avon Preservation Committee on the future of the market town 'on which fortune has settled an incomparable distinction', and in particular on proposals for new factories within the borough. These would assuredly be manned 'by immigration'. Existing townsfolk were not suffering undue stress because of the lack of factory employment; indeed, 'if an occasional youth discovers a mechanical bent, it is no great hardship to him to migrate to a neighbouring

---

* Stratford-upon-Avon: Report on Future Development, 1923. Prepared at the instance of the Stratford-upon-Avon Preservation Committee; published by permission of Stratford-upon-Avon Corporation.

town'. As for more comfortably established citizens who might be tempted by the prospect of financial profit, they were warned that this would be offset by a rise in rates and in population, which would necessitate 'housing schemes, schools, and a rapid expansion of all the usual municipal services'.

There was really little doubt how the town's establishment, heavy with shopkeepers and estate agents and retired professionals, would feel about such expansion. Nor does it come as much of a surprise to find that in Stratford between the wars social barriers were as strong as ever. Mass education had yet to make much impact on the lower working class. Indeed, Mary's school (in which, ironically, so much of her life was to be spent) seemed to have changed very little since her father's day, in the 1880s. 'Grammar school boys' were beings from another planet. A girl's position in this society could be placed exactly: her clothes, her diet, her home address, what she did in her leisure time, all these things gave her away. Above all, after thirteen, it was where she worked.

Amongst Mary's teenage contemporaries in the 1930s, to be a shop assistant was, apart from marriage, the ultimate career goal, achieved only by a select and envied few. There was one ray of hope in this attitude: by the time she found herself on the labour market, at the very bottom of her list and everyone else's was domestic service. An elder sister had already rejected 'service' in favour of factory work, where 'you knows when you's a-goin to start an when you's a-goin to finish. And you gets your money on Friday night.'*

The Stratford accent, with undertones of the receding countryside, was another give-away. But there was a directness, an earthiness of manner, about this new class of working girls, a certain cockiness, that was slightly alarming. Notwithstanding the reports of preservation committees and the Shakespeare lobby and the ratepayers' lobby, new factories *had* come to Stratford, and these girls, who a generation earlier might have been skivvies in private households, isolated and vulnerable, helped to keep industry going. During the Second World War they *did* keep it going, although in 1945 the authorities were swift to hint at a time limit to their new-found freedoms. Of the canning factory where Mary worked as mechanic's mate, a local newspaper wrote: 'By the end of the hostilities with Germany, the firm [Stratford-on-Avon Produce Canners Ltd] had dispatched the magnificent total of 40 million cans of fruit, vegetables, soups and jams to our fighting forces . . . Much credit is due

* *The Dillen*, p. 162.

to the work of the women and girls who took the places of men called to military service.'*

In the factories they found for the first time a sort of collective voice, albeit the possibility of formal organization never seems to have occurred to Mary, for one. She does not mention trade unions, possibly because although working conditions were poor, sometimes downright dangerous, pay was comparatively good. The collective voice manifested itself rather in comradeliness (new to the women's workplace, if not to the community at large), in a lack of deference, and in 'having a good laugh' at the boss on every possible occasion. There was also (notably during the war) the chance of job satisfaction.

Now and then, outside work situations, the business-owning and professional class which controlled the town's government met the lower working class socially. As Mary observed (in direct contrast to an ecstatic account of a garden party for brewery workers at 'The Hill' in the local press), such meetings were not always 'a success': a reminder that viewpoint is all-important. Occasionally, marriage broke through the barriers. But on the whole, working girls with over-ambitious social aspirations, or even with dim yearnings fanned by the cinema (especially the American cinema) for *something*, were, like Mary, doomed to meet their come-uppance. If 'the worst' happened, some families rallied round. In others, especially where the parents had social aspirations too, the shame was overwhelming. The luckless daughter was sent away, or declared to be 'morally defective' and committed to a local asylum, her child to adoption. Today, in 1984, some of these girls, now old women, institution-alized and dull of speech, are still being discovered by vigilant social workers, or in one case by a long-grieving son: a living testimony to social attitudes in the 1930s and 1940s.

Mary, I am glad to say, tells a different tale. Compassion and love did triumph, sometimes, in spite of society. So for those who like happy endings, there is one; for those who like to wonder . . . well, who is to say what happiness is? It took courage for her to tell what must in part be a tribute to some of the people she met along the way. Most of these I have left with their real names; a few still living have been given pseudonyms, to protect their anonymity. On first men-tion, but not thereafter, this is indicated in the text. No claim is made for the tale as social history, although as a record of feelings and attitudes rather than historical events there may be something of

* *Stratford-on-Avon Herald*, 25 May 1945.

interest to the historian. Spoken recollection has flaws as well as richnesses. I offer no apology for what is no more and no less than any of us might do without the aid of reference books or original documents, or with very little formal education, and I hope that others will be encouraged to pick up their tape recorders (or even pencils) before it is too late, and preserve some of the treasure that lies within every family.

A. H.

Friday's dream
Saturday told
Will come true
Though ever so old

Though I am old with wandering
Through hollow lands and hilly lands,
I will find out where she has gone,
And kiss her lips and take her hands;
And walk among long dappled grass,
And pluck till time and times are done
The silver apples of the moon,
The golden apples of the sun.

W. B. Yeats

Emma ('our Mother') outside 20 Park Road,
Stratford-upon-Avon, c.1919

Chapter One

When I shut my eyes I can see us all sat round the fire at number 20 Park Road, laughing. Mostly we was rowing at our house, but I do remember even our Mother laughed, that night. I was sat by her feet, and Dad was there, another wonder, and Jess and Flo—she hadn't gone into service then—and our Else and Ede and Cyril and Jim, even George—he was on leave from the Flying Corps—everybody. The pig was on the hearth.

Where he'd come from I don't know. There he was, in the best place of all, wrapped in an old khaki coat—it was Dad's old greatcoat, I 'spect, from the army—and there he *wasn't*!

'E's vanished!'

'Stuck!'

'Oh God!'

'Mam e's stuck up sleeve!'

'Don't sit there gawpin—go an get the scissors!'

Our Else was helpless with laughing, so was Ede. In the end, as usual, Jess went.

Dad chuckled: 'It minds me of the time . . .'

We knew we was in for a story. Then 'Phew!' went the little pig as Jess cut him out. He fell back, onto the coat, righted himself and went 'Phew!' again.

'Did I ever tell you,' said Dad, 'when *I* was small, ow I walked to Warwick an back once for a dillen pig, just like this little fella?'

*

That was the last time we were all together, *family*. So many things happened. I was the youngest, four years old, and Park Road was the size of my world: two rows of council houses, council cottages they were called then, with long backs full of cabbages and pigs and fowl—and kiddies! The road didn't lead anywhere, it just petered out into a field and a steep bank and a railway.

It was a busy line, a lot of trains went by. We had them all night as well, shunting and doing. You could hear them in your sleep. Clanging in the sidings, pushing up that hill from Stratford towards Brum, push and puff, one engine at the back, one on the front: push 'n' puff, push 'n' puff. If the wind was right you could hear a train coming miles away, and the whistle! Oh the excitement when you heard that whistle!

Else (in cook's hat) and Jess (front) with friend in Red Horse yard, Stratford-upon-Avon, c.1920

When a troop train came through we all turned out! You never seen so many kiddies! Swarming down those passages, running for the field. Most families up Park Road had eight or ten; a lot had other folks' families lodging with them, young marrieds, and they had kiddies too. I was good at running but sometimes I was slowed down

cos our Else had suddenly got the idea of *taking* me to see the trains.
It was nice at first, I liked the fuss; then it started to annoy me.
She was my eldest sister, seventeen. She worked at the Red Horse
so she thought she was something, and very bossy. Why she wanted
to be wading through the bottom field with us kiddies—it was always
flooded, that field—Heaven knows. But our family was noted for
being unpredictable.

There was plenty of time to get to the bottom of the embankment,
even with our Else in tow: the trains couldn't go fast, *they* had to slow
down and all. From Park Road into the town they were slowing
down. We could see the driver and his fireman, see the red hot glow,
feel it! And the soldiers! They hung from the windows and they
shouted and waved, and out of the sky came hurtling corned beef
tins, quite big uns, medium size, you had to watch your head—and
biscuits. Praps they'd got fed up with them. At any rate, rolling down
the bank they came, lovely corned beef and biscuits, and hundreds of
kiddies fighting for them, me included.

'Come on Else!' I cried.

I didn't linger; you grabbed what you could. I was small, but I was
quite aggressive. I'd come back with a tin, maybe, if I was lucky, and I
always got some biscuits. They were big square uns, hard, ever so
hard, just like dog biscuits. Looked like one and all, that colour.

'Ugh,' said Else.

'I gotta *tin*!'

I could picture our Mother's face. But then I saw our Else was in a
bad mood, you know, whipping the heads off the flowers, scowling.

'Us'll wait for next un,' she said.

I couldn't believe it! 'I gotta *tin*!'

All the kiddies were rushing home. I knowed there wouldn't be
another troop train that day; there never was.

'Come on Else!'

'You can bloomin well wait 'ere with me,' she said, 'you selfish
little bugger.'

She was in a flaming mood.

*

If you'd asked me who was the most important person in Stratford
I'd a-said: '*Mrs Windsor*!' They lived further up the road than us, the
Windsors, and she was the only one with a mangle. She used to
mangle our clothes for us—no charge! I often took our mangling up
to her, and the school towels. Dad was caretaker at the Church

school, and every Friday we had to wash all the towels, fifty or so of them, and the dusters. She was a very good woman, Mrs Windsor; even though she looked like a gypsy, and that was my big dread, gypsies, I liked her very much.

We went to her for everything. 'Cup o' sugar, Missus Windsor?' 'Bit o' tea, Missus Windsor?' Even for home-made wine: you took your own rhubarb. But most of all we went to her for *money*. You could always be sure she'd have some. What she did was insure her kiddies—Beryl 'n' Norman 'n' Ernie 'n' Sid 'n' Freddie, he was called Flash, 'n' Ivy 'n' Lol 'n' Myrtle—had insurances on them for so many years. She had so much in, see, had so much out, and *we* borrowed off her, for a penny or twopence.

'Mam says: "Can we 'ave two bob, Missus Windsor, just till er gets er wages?" '

She writ it all down on the wall, who owed her, and how much was left to pay: 'GARDINER' 'HEWINS'.

There was a Mr Windsor. He was very handsome, well, I used to think so, with a little moustache, but sort of insignificant besides her. He was always falling off his bike. He'd get on again, keep falling off; lean on it, push it. It was impossible for him to *ride* it. I used to wonder why it was he could never stay on his bike. Years later, after the Abdication, they became the Duke and Duchess of Park Road.

Myrtle, their youngest, had a club foot; Flash had a cock eye. That was unlucky—unlucky for me. When I started school he threw stones at me, every day. I don't know why he frit me so—praps there's always got to be another kiddie you're scared of, at that age— he was little, littler'n me, fat. Anyway, he showered these stones at me as I came from school, and I was frit to death! By the canal, up the Brum Road, there's a dip and a gate and there *he'd* be, laying in wait. 'Flash' we called him, Flash Windsor, and that's what he was: *sly*. He'd be waiting for me, every day. Now I think: why ever didn't I tell our Jim? But when you're small, when you're a kiddie, it's a different world. Like Park Road—look at it now!

Mrs Windsor was the most important; our Mother was the most beautiful. And once—I think . . . Well, it was the worst row we'd ever had in our house. I felt, you know, really afraid, sick, much worse'n Flash Windsor chucking stones.

She never had a 'best friend'. She didn't like folks popping in and out, much, she said it was asking for trouble. So she didn't have any special acquaintances, only the Sweets on Brum Road. Now it happened that Hilda Sweet got married and she went to Leicester. Our Mother got quite friendly with hers.

She said: 'Hilda's invited me for weekend.'

'Ey?'

'I'm a-goin to Leicester for weekend and I've got my ticket.' The echo said: 'Just you try 'n' stop me!'

'You sure you ain't got summat else 'n' all,' said Dad, 'like a fancy man?'

He shouted, there was a big row, but she went. She went and left us all behind. I can still remember the fear: it was worse'n when Ede lost me at the Mop. I thought: She ain't comin back!

Sunday afternoon, Dad took me to the LMS station. He'd been wounded in the war, Dad, he was a cripple; he had to go with a stick, so it was a slow trip. He didn't get a pension, well, he'd took the lump sum. Sometimes when they were rowing our Mother would say bitterly: '*Lump sum!* The bloody army must be laughin its bloody head off!' and he'd shout back: 'Oo spent it, I'd like to know?'

I'd seen his wound once, when she was bathing him. He came home covered in coal dust, and chalk, and she bathed him by the fire. When she was bathing him, or me, or anybody, our Mother always kept the others out, but one day I rushed in and I *saw*. Horrible. He was covered in scars, and one side of him, low down, where there should a-been flesh, there was—nothing. You could see the bone! I'd guessed it would be horrible, like the butcher's shop. I'd seen his washing in the bucket, all blood and stuff, every day his clothes were put in to soak, but till you've really *seen* . . . How could our Mother bear to touch him? And every day, well it seemed like every day to me, he was drunk.

This Sunday afternoon, I will say that, he'd stayed sober. We watched every train come in, every last passenger go. By now I was in the grip of terror—and who knows what was going on in Dad's head? He kept asking the chap at the station about trains from Leicester, over and over again. Then—it seemed like the very last train—out she got. Oh the relief!

He started shouting: 'You *bin* with somebody!'

She hugged me to death, nearly. The feel of her! That lovely safe smell of Cologne! She had a lot of Cologne for her heads. Dad and her seemed quite pleased to see each other, even though he was shouting and raving and that. I couldn't make it out. I'd never seen him hit her once, and she never hit him. She was a big woman, our Mother, bigger'n him, a powerful big woman, she could a-done, cos when she was roused she had a temper and a half. She could shift a copper on her own, though she wasn't as strong as she'd used to be. 'You should a-seen me then,' she said. At the station she just shouted back: 'You're an ole pot, you is! A-callin me black!' and 'Oh shut up!' That's all she said.

Emma, early 1920s: taken at Leicester during her first (and only) escape from home

Later she showed us a photograph she'd had took at Leicester. She looked just like she did when she got out the train—Flo sent that hat, from London, she'd gone to work for Jews—beautiful. I never did know where the necklace came from, or where it went. She never wore it, after. It was like a little new moon. I'd gaze and gaze at that photograph and wonder. Maybe Dad did the same. Did she do it to teach him a lesson? Whatever the truth of it, she never went again.

*

That trip to Leicester seemed to start it off. 'Flo's gone to London, Mam went to *Leicester*!' That was the chant. 'Why can't *I*?' Not to

6

her face, of course, just clucks and grumbles, like the start of a fight in the hen run. Oh God, I thought, another big row. Only words, here and there, then, suddenly . . . Else did it first. Half a mile up the road, that's all, but it was a start. She took a living-in job, at Bishopton. It was even nearer the railway than Park Road; the trains ran through the kitchen, practically. When I went up to see her I thought: Praps she'll be satisfied now!

Our Jim said: 'Did you see a motorbike in the bushes at Bishopton? An *engine-driver* on a *motorbike?*'

Flo was in London, as I said. And Ede fell for the drummer in the town band.

I woke up one morning and my guardians were gone. You'd a-thought it would have made a very big difference to my life, at home, everywhere, but it didn't! Else and Ede kept coming back; they might as well still a-lived at our house. In and out, in and out, asking our Mother's advice, bossing me about, gossiping. And there was still four in our bed. That was three too many, as far as I was concerned.

Chapter Two

'Sides to middle!'our Mother would say. That meant another sheet was going home; the sides had to be put together, joined up. So it was *Sides to middle!* My heart sank when I heard those three words. You had to lay on a ridge, then. Our George always had a bedroom on his own. There was Jim and Cyril at the top of our bed, and who was at the bottom with me? It must have been Jess. Well, even the *prospect* of George going opened up a new horizon.

This is how it happened. He fell in love.

'I'd like you all to meet—Miss De Bonelli!'

We stared. Her dress was covered with millions of tiny beads, all sparkling beads and tinsel. I thought she was lovely. But when they'd gone, our Else was there and she giggled and she said: 'Er's from Fossett's, *I* reckon!'

Fossett's Circus came every year to Stratford; they lodged at the Green Dragon.

You could see our Mother was a bit upset. It was so unexpected. George never stepped out of line, he always toed it. She was even more upset next week when they turned up carrying a violin!

'Miss De Bonelli can play. Er's goin to teach me ow to do it—upstairs.'

Up they went, and from our George's bedroom, from the ceiling, came this awful noise: *Eeeh! Eeeh!*

Dad said, 'Oo's learnin oo?' Our Mother was dumbstruck. Well, she'd always given George preferential treatment; he'd always done what he liked. He was the eldest, out of the Flying Corps, apprenticed to a Stratford printer. George had to have a room to himself; George had to have a back leg on Sundays. Being the youngest I had the head. Imagine, a rabbit's head, the little tongue in still! I ate it. 'Course I did. They say that's how I came to have the gift of the gab, eating all those little tongues; I don't know.

The result was, our George had always been one to himself, thought he was a cut above the rest of us. He was *glovey*, wore kid

8

gloves, a proper toff. He was the toffiest chap on Park Road. The Windsors used to call 'Glovey!' after him, but he was alright to me.

Sat'day dinner time, one o'clock, I always went up the Brum Road to meet him, and always he'd got a penny or a ha'penny for me. You could buy a lot for a penny: kali suckers, sherbet. I liked anything in the sweet line.

His pal laughed and said: ' 'Ere she comes!'

But Sat'day night! I paid for it then! We all had to sit there while Marg performed—that was her other name, *Margery*. She seemed nice. It was just that violin—she couldn't do a blooming note right—and her clothes! I thought her clothes were lovely, but the others didn't half pull her to bits, 'specially Else and Ede:

'Did you *see*?'

'Oo didn't?'

'I thought I'd *die*!'

Even our Mother joined in: 'That wench should be on top a Christmas tree.'

George said: 'Miss De Bonelli's goin to give you a *selection*.'

Marg started up. *Eeeh*! *Eeeh*! And our Else starts laughing. She started up her sleeve but she couldn't stop. I felt a giggle coming. I nearly wet my knickers trying to hold it in, and I was glad I did cos George gave Else such a slap across the face.

When they'd gone, Dad—he'd kept quiet, he'd never said a word—he said: 'Er name's *Bonehill*. And er comes from ————.' It was one of the villages. You could have knocked us all down with a feather.

'Ow do you know?'

'Oh I know,' he said.

But he went on calling her Miss De Bonelli, even if we never, after that. When he wanted, Dad could be a perfect gentleman. He'd just chuckle afterwards, to himself.

*

When the talleyman came for his money—we used to have all our shoes off him—our Mother said: ' 'Ide! 'Ide under the table!'

She locked the door.

Somebody'd say, 'E's comin!' or: 'I's seen im, Brum Road!'

We always knew when the talleyman was coming, or the insurance. That was only sixpence a week, Fridays, a matter of sixpence, but our Mother was borrowing, all the time! Sixpence was a lot to her. Under the table we went: everybody, our Mother 'n' Dad too if they were in the kitchen, cos we had a back way, people could get round the back. If the insurance caught her, he caught her sometimes, she'd say: 'Well I don't know what you's a-moanin about—it ain't a debt!'

She told him off, as if it was his fault she couldn't pay! He started stammering: 'Alright then missus, we'll leave it till next week.'

Then there was the school attendance officer. Jim never went to school much, he went running round Wells' back. There was a good passage there, see, between the houses. He hid round there while our Mother told the lies. She had to do that. He wasn't well, she used to say, things like that.

We had to keep a watch out for all sorts of people, according to the day.

But once a month, the last day of every month, Dad got paid! He took us for a treat: me and our Cyril and my best friend Sis Wells. The Wells lived opposite—they were eleven—and Sis Wells was my best friend throughout our lives. Dad always took us to the fish 'n' chip shop on Rother Street!

They had benches and a wooden table, well, not a proper table, a trestle. You could see the Fountain through the window. Eating out—we loved that! We sat there and the chips spat and crackled in the fat, they *talked*!

'We'll soon be done!'

The smell! We sat there slavering, you know, like three Jack Russells round a rabbit hole. I think Dad got his entertainment watching *us*! They served the chips to you, on a plate. Salt and vinegar . . . ready . . . set . . . *go*!

Sis said: 'Our Bomber's got a horse for 'is cart!' He had a fruit and veg round.

I said: 'Our Jess's got a tiny little babby!'

Dad looked! Then he laughed and said: 'That's right!'

Oh the taste of those chips!

Every night when she got into bed I used to stare at Jess. Her belly was swelled, huge, like a pumpkin. It grew and grew. I knowed she was going to have a baby, she'd told me, but I thought it would burst out. In some ways I was quite innocent. I used to lie in bed waiting for the *pop*!

'I missed it!' I said. It was my one big regret.

Dad seemed upset.

' 'Ave some pop, you three,' he said, ' 'Ave a blow out. 'Ere—'ave some pop!'

And he bought us a whole bottle between us! That's how Jess's baby came to be mixed up in my mind with lemonade.

Our Mother chose the names. She said, 'E's goin to be called after the Prince o' Wales.'
We called him Bert. He looked so unhappy.

*

You'll notice I haven't mentioned my education. The fact is, I can't remember anything about school much, 'cept cleaning it. I'd been helping to clean it since I was a little girl, four or five years old; we *all* had, cos as I said, Dad was a cripple and our Mother—well, she was a big woman, lovely looking, but she was weighed down by the biggest rupture you've ever seen. So by the time I was thirteen I knew every nook and cranny of that school, every gas mantle, every rat hole, every ledge where the bloody dust gathered. Oh the coal dust and the chalk! It's a wonder it hadn't killed us all.

I wasn't good at anything else—'cept outside games. I couldn't write proper, add up. I don't think I was dim, I just thought: There must be better things to do'n this! You could see the teachers thought the same. Some of them, like Miss Farmer, had been there years; they'd grown old and fat so they *hit* you, never moved from their chair, just called you up to the front and gave you a swipe across the head. And the young one! We used to be praps at netball in the front yard, and Miss Salt the young teacher, she always wore a very short gym slip. Up and up she jumped, up and up; she loved jumping! She didn't pay much attention to us, cos by this time a big crowd had gathered on the pavement: chaps going by to the station, the boys from the Commercial school on their way to games. There were whistles and shouts. We never realized it was Miss Salt's limbs, and her lovely attire. *Then* we thought it was us, in our navy blue knickers. But really it was Miss Salt, jumping and jumping; she was the great attraction.

The Vicar came round regular. We all stood up for him, all at once; the classrooms were partitioned with glass, you could see through the whole school. He walked through—if you didn't curtsey you got a swipe off the teacher, after—and then we were allowed to sit down. I used to think: 'Why's e come?' and 'What's it all for?' For example, I weren't too bad at needlework, but you never *made* anything. All you did was stitches, different sorts of fancy stitches, and then you had to unpick them and do some more, with the same bit o' stuff. Naturally, it got black as your hat. Then there was *Empire Day*. They planned weeks in advance for that. The teacher said: 'Hewins— Jamaican Banana!' My friend Betty who married Joe Shakespeare was a Tasmanian Apple. Sis? She was lucky; she went to the Board school.

Hockey team, Church of England School, Stratford-upon-Avon, late 1920s: Mary second row, far right, in a smart turn-out that says much for her mother's ingenuity (the tie was knitted)

Our mothers did their best: we all had something on our heads, like Christmas crackers. You can imagine some of the boys! Their faces! I had a shift with '*BANANA*' on it, made out of wrapping paper; Betty had cardboard. When the great day came we paraded in the front yard. I was dying of embarrassment. Somebody whispered I'd got '*BANANA*' spelled wrong; I hadn't o' course, but I believed them. We was marched around, then one by one we stood on a platform with a Union Jack draped across, and streamers.

I had to say: 'I'm a Jamaican banana.' I felt like one and all. For once I prayed the boys from the Commercial school wouldn't come by. If anyone giggled they got a swipe. Miss Farmer hit very hard. She leant over the piano stool and she hit you as you marched past. She'd got it off to a fine art.

Once, I remember, I'd done a sum wrong, so I put a cross. That wouldn't a-been so bad if I'd left it, but I put this cross hard on the paper, ever so hard, spoilt the page. 'You spoilt the page!' she shouted. I got a swipe over the head for that. 'You spoilt your *book*!' That was exaggerating, but you couldn't argue with the teachers, you couldn't even reason with them. So you can imagine how I was longing and longing for Christmas, when I was fourteen.

*

For the last and the thousandth time Miss Farmer went *Ping*! ''Ere's your note!' And we all sang 'God Save the King'. Then she said: 'Today we 'ave to wish Mary Hewins well in er new career.'

Career! Two of the girls were smirking; they'd got their names down at J. C. Smith's the Draper's. Oh they thought they were something, those two girls. Later, some of the others went to Woolworth's; Woolworth's was coming to Stratford—'*EVERY-THING IN ITS PLACE NOTHING OVER SIXPENCE!*'—and when it did, all the girls who were clever, but not clever enough for Smith's, they went there for interview. It was hard to get in; well, the ones they picked were a better class'n me. I wouldn't a-stood a chance.

I wasn't dressed like them in those days: we'd got more fleas'n clothes in our house!

I'd wake Jess up: 'Ey Jess! There's a flea in bed!'

We lit a candle, tried to catch it. Once you know there's a flea, you can't stop. If it gets you first it'll mark you so's everybody knows. They could tell at school if you'd got fleas: the marks were all round your blooming neck. Mostly they bite on your neck. The girl behind you . . . oh God.

My looks were alright, but you'd got to be—well, a bit posher. J. C. Smith's could take their pick. And Woolworth's, when they opened. Dora went, and Madge—she was a teacher, after—and the Bromley girls. The Bromleys lived at 'Glencoe', in Arden Street, by the school, one of those big houses. They took in lodgers. Madge's Dad was only a baker but they were a bit superior. Woolworth's seemed to go for that type of girl.

I told myself I wouldn't a-liked it, anyway. As for service, well, that had been suggested! One of the teachers said: 'I think you might be suited to domestic service, Hewins.' Little did she know I'd already done enough service at home to last me a lifetime—*and* at school! Who dusted the classrooms? Washed the partitions down? Who did she think cleared up after her? As the others left home, George and Else and Ede and Flo and Jim—one after another to get married they'd left home and were gone—there was only me and Jess left to do the school at night. Jess was a little 'put on', but she'd never been strong. Most of it fell on me.

No, I thought, you can stuff service.

It boiled down to the brewery. The brewery was the only place, really, for girls like us. But there was a list! There was even a waiting list for the *brewery*, you had to have your name put down! Sis was accepted. Her Dad wasn't 'church', he was the only one on Park Road who voted Labour, so you can imagine how he got laughed at! And he sent Sis to the Board school. The result was she'd had a better education 'n me. She was accepted, and I wasn't! The brewery turned me down. It was a nasty shock.

Sis said: 'Never mind, Mary, it'll come up,' meaning my name, 'bound to.'

I remember I thought: They think I'm not good enough.

*

There was nothing for it but the Alum. I went to the Aluminium Factory on Brum Road and they said: 'Yes, you can start.'

I was buffing up the pans and kettles and things, with a duster, shining them up when they came from the polishers. You got filthy—*black*! It got on your hands, on your face. And you went home filthy; there weren't no washroom. You had to walk home looking like that—one o'clock on Sat'days, in broad daylight! I used always to be glancing at my face in the bottom of the kettles, to check.

'Oh God, it's on for the day now!' or if it was clean, if I'd escaped: 'Am I prettier'n er? What does *e* think of me?'

There was quite a reflection, you see, and as the chaps went by, well, you wanted to look nice. You could see yourself in the saucepans too, but not so well. One boy I fancied, his name was Harry, he was from Warwick. They used to bring them to the Alum in charas, men and women, from all over. They couldn't get enough from Stratford—not like the brewery, no strangers got in *there*. Well, all the girls at the Alum were set to cut one another out over Harry! But I was the one who got friendly with him! I used to gaze and gaze in the bottom of the kettle and think: If my clothes ain't much my *face* is alright!

But I pined for the brewery. Sis was there, all my friends, Jess and our Jim. Early every morning the brewery hooter went, you could hear it all over Stratford, and I used to feel so out of it. I was terribly jealous of Sis, though I never let on. We were still best friends. And at fourteen, with the world in front of you . . . I didn't stay down for long!

Chapter Three

One day I said to Sis or Sis said to me: 'Let's get fancy garters!'

So we did. They were lovely, ruched ribbon and elastic, with a bell. Mine was bright green; that was my colour then. You could have two bells, but Sis said two was overdoing it. We put them on in the toilet up our yard, so's our mothers wouldn't suspect—well, once you'd got them on, you can imagine, it was jingle, jingle, jingle—and we set off for town.

There was nothing else to do, nothing else you could afford to do! We thought we were the sexiest things in Stratford: dresses up at the front, a dip in the back so's the garter showed when you moved, just a bit, burnt cork on our eyebrows, a dab of powder, high heels! I was in agony most of the time, what with the shoes and the binder. I had to wear it, to flatten me. I was slim, I'd got slim hips, but oh God! My bust! Your figure had to be *straight*, you see, and my bust had grown that big. Sis was lucky, but all our family was big busted; we took after our Mother, I 'spect. I used to think: 'If only I hadn't got this bloody bust I'd get er chaps!' Sis used to get better chaps'n me; well, I used to think so. She seemed to get the pick. She'd get the best one, what *I* thought was the best one!

We walked anyhow till we got to the Fountain; we almost ran, cos we knowed we'd got to be back before nine, before it got dark, cos there weren't no lamps much, up Park Road. When we got to the Fountain we slowed up, we started walking proper: down along Wood Street, Bridge Street, down along the 'croft. That's where we made for—the *Bancroft*!

There were wooden steps there, then, with a little bridge, where the wharf was. We went *up* the steps: watch-each-step-mind-your-heels-don't-catch-keep-your-head-up! You try doing that! Walk-along-like-Lady Muck-and-*down*-the-other-side.

'They're 'ere!' said Sis.

There they were, right as the mail: Eddie 'n' Jack in their brown blazers and cream flannel trousers.

'What oh,' said Eddie.

'What oh,' said Jack.

They used to dress alike, we thought they were brothers for ages. They came from country, 'specially for it, every Sat'day. Well, we put the brakes on then, we went really slow, I can tell you—they was attractive chaps—had a bit of a chat. That's all we did: *talk*. Then we went on, towards the Tram. That was our walk: down as far as the old Tramway then back again, with them watching—we hoped! Well, you could feel it, if you'd made an impression; and then of course we pretended we couldn't care less.

My trouble was, I always made the biggest impression when I wasn't trying. Sure as fate, there was Dick, and his friend Eric. Eric was a great tall chap and Dick was little and dark. He didn't wait for you, Dick, he *lurked*. He wasn't a tramp, but nearly; he worked on the fields and he always wore a long raincoat and a funny cap. He loved me from afar.

'Oh heck!' I said.

But I was pleased to see him, really, cos he walked from Clifford, every Sat'day, to bring me a bar of chocolate. He was that shy, Dick, looked all sawney* at me, held the chocolate out at arm's length, a half pound bar! Cadbury's Milk!

'Frightened you'll bite,' Sis said.

All of a sudden, he *flung* it at me! I took it—and we ran! I thought: It is wrapped up!

We didn't stop till we got half way up Sheep Street. We weren't half puffing and panting.

Sis said: 'You goin?'

'Where?'

'Puntin wi them two.'

Yes! It was what you might call a *break through*. Jack and Eddie had asked us to meet them next Sat'day to go punting on the river!

*

Just my luck, I got Eddie. He was the quiet one; well, he always left the talking to Jack, butter wouldn't melt in his mouth. I thought: This is goin to be bloomin boring. They were alright *together*, if you

---

* Sheepish, foolish.

17

know what I mean, but seeing them separate . . . Praps they thought the same. I'd got my new green suede shoes on.

Well, Sis and Jack set off down river towards the Theatre, and that's when I got my first surprise. Eddie pushed off *up* river, towards the bathing place.

'Ain't we followin them?'

'Two's company.' He winked at me.

'What's wrong with your eye? You got a fly in it or summat?' I ignored all the hints.

When we got to Bird's Corner he drew into the bank and said: 'This is it! The end of the line!' Wink wink.

He pulled in and jumped out and left me to manage best I could. He was a real gentleman.

'You jokin?' I could see he wasn't.

He said: 'You don't think I'm goin back there and 'ave to pay for this bleedin boat do you?'

Well! I *called* him! It didn't do much good. He went up by those private houses, but I was too proud to follow. I set off across the fields. Squelch, squelch! It was thick mud. My shoes! You should have seen them; they were ruined. I thought: What'll I *do*? Our Mother'll 'ave a fit if she finds out where I've been! It was only the second time on.

Fortunately, that very day Dad found a pound note in the pub. You see, every morning after the school he cleaned the Green Dragon opposite, swept it up, did the toilet. I wheedled ten bob out of him and I went to Brum and bought another pair of shoes, exactly the same. You'd a-thought it would have taught me a lesson: beauty is only skin deep. It didn't, o' course!

Chapter Four

I'd been at the Alum six months. Then one day, I shall never forget it because of all that happened since—you could say on that day the wheels were set in motion and there was no turning back—Sis came running to the factory door. I can see her now, in her clogs, and everybody's astonishment.

'*Mary*!' she shouted. Even at fifteen she'd got a big mouth, Sis had. 'Mary yer name's up!'

You might wonder why I was so excited about starting at the brewery. I was soon wondering myself. It weren't light work, not like the Alum. There was broken glass all over the place. I was a washer, at the bottling end. That's where the women were. I had to wash the bottles when they came back from the pubs, smell them, guess what some dirty bugger had put in them. You'd be surprised— paraffin, piss, all sorts—*ugh*! You nearly heaved, every time. It was terrible. You had to smell each bottle; you could be smelling all day at the back of the washing machine. It made you feel sick; sometimes I *was*.

I noticed Kate always had to wash the stoppers. That was pretty heavy work; buckets of stoppers are heavy to keep carrying. Poor Kate, she always had to do that. Jack Timms the foreman decided; he decided everything. I suppose he thought cos Kate was big 'n' strong . . . She had a fatter sister who was on the washing too; she had to wash the bottles as long as I can remember. That was a rotten job, washing the bottles, wet and horrible.

I was moved a bit higher up: I was on the bottling machine. You put the bottles on and you changed every half hour; another girl stood by you and took the bottles off and put the stoppers in. That was the worst job of all, tightening the stoppers, cos sometimes the bottle broke and then your hand would go. You had a strap on your hand, a big thick strap with an iron thing in the middle with spikes. It had got to grip that stopper. But if something went wrong . . . *Aaagh*!

And then the bottles went round and you sat down and labelled. The next girl put them in cases, and so on. We changed round every half hour. We didn't have a break, but if the washers didn't keep up with us we *had* to have a bit of a rest, we had to shut the machine off then!

Phew!

It was different at the brewery, and not just the work—a lot o' the chaps was *drunk*! I'd seen men drunk often enough, well, Dad was drunk Sunday dinner time regular, but at the brewery they was always drunk! It shook me at first. They were allowed so much a day, see, the men were, and they could pinch as much as they wanted, drink it on the spot, dip a bucket in. They said they had to sample it! They were never sober. You should a-seen them rolling home breakfast time: drunk in charge of push bikes, a lot of them.

I was earning fourteen and six a week, and I had to give our Mother twelve. That left half-a-crown. We went roller skating at the Hippodrome; in the summer we went dancing in the Bancroft Gardens, to the Town Band. Well—'dancing'! We thought we could, but we couldn't, really. Kate was the dancer. As I said, she was fat, so she danced with her sister—but she was a brilliant dancer! We just sort of scuffled around, waltzes, that sort o' thing—but Kate! She was light as a bird. Sis and me practised the Charleston on Park Road, when we got home. We'd try it, show off, in the street. But Kate was the dancer. You wouldn't a-thought it possible, would you?

With our spending money we bought face powder and high heeled shoes, Woodbines. It was Sis taught me to smoke. We shut ourselves in the toilet. She said: 'You want to try one!' I did. I wonder if smoking killed her? You paid twopence for a packet of Woodbines, but generally I pinched Cyril's. He smoked a lot, sent Bert down to the shop for them. I'd waylay him and take one out.

Cyril got so annoyed! 'Do they only sell fags in bloody *nines*, now?'

He weren't like Jim—Jim was generous, he'd give you half of what he had and that was never very much—our Cyril ranted and raved.

So picture my surprise, my *face*, when he said: 'Ow should you like some new clothes? For brewery trip?'

I thought: 'Bugger me!'

He said: 'Well I can't 'ave my sister disgracin us.'

He gave me *two pound*!

'Don't go askin for no more,' he said, 'cos you won't get it.'

*

Sis and me had been planning our outfit for months, what we'd wear, down to the last detail. We sat on the railings at the end of our road, scrunching apples and discussing it. That was our entertainment, after work: chatting, watching the traffic—charabancs, a car, lots o' bikes . . .

'Look at *im!*' said Sis.

He was cycling along the Brum Road. Every day five o'clock sharp he cycled past in his blazer and his tie and his posh cap, and every day from the railings there we watched him. He never looked, but he knew we was watching alright. You could *tell*. He used to turn colour a bit, blush, push down on those pedals to get past us, fast, faster and faster.

'Ya ya grammar school boy!'

It was windy cos leaves from the apple trees kept falling in our hair and he was struggling so with his bike. That bike! Oh he had a lovely bike—and bright cheeks from the weather. And just at that minute— his cap blowed off! We jumped down and ran out and grabbed it! We threw it over the railings into Schofield's orchard.

'That's got rid of im!' said Sis.

'Did you see 'is *'air?*'

' 'Is *what?*'

We laughed! But his hair! It was the colour of autumn; it was dark red, gold. I thought he was like nobody I'd ever seen: beautiful.

'Sis—e can't go *no*where without 'is cap!'

'That's the idea!'

I said, it came out, I hadn't meant to say it but it just came out: 'E's different.'

'Stuck up you mean.'

'Where's e live? I wonder where e's goin?'

Sis said: 'Give me a proper chap, any day.'

I thought: If she means that Dougie . . . But I kept it to myself. Sis was my friend, but I was always frightened of her mouth.

'Talkin of red—what 'bout *hats?*' she said.

That got me laughing again.

In the end we decided on bright orange. 'Course I'd been thinking all along I wouldn't be able to afford it! The Wells had more money'n us—well, they always seemed richer. One of her brothers, Harry, he worked in the Sale Yard, picked up fruit and veg on the side; another un, Bomber Wells, went out with his cart, *redistributed* it. Folks on Park Road used to have to buy stuff off him; though in our case I don't know that we ever paid for it, cos our Mother never paid anybody much. She wasn't what you'd call good with money.

When there was a rummage sale our Mother always came back with fancy cushions. She didn't need them; well, you can't do anything *with* them, can you? She got as many fancy cushions as she could; Mrs Wells got nice woollies and that. 'Course, none of them paid, they just said: 'I'll see if it fits,' or 'if this colour goes,' and passed it to the back. That was it! They'd got it!

Mrs Wells went to Mitchell's and got them to save her cakes, regular, the ones that had gone stale. She planned in advance; our Mother never did. She was more—*on the spur of the moment*. The Wells always seemed to have those lovely doughnuts and cream horns and things on the table. When I went over there Mrs Wells used to give me one.

' 'Elp yourself Mary love.'

I thought that was wonderful! *We* never had any cake!

Sis was as thrilled as me 'bout Cyril's unexpected present.

'We can match now! Like we planned!'

I said: 'We'll go to Smith's!'

So we did. We went to J. C. Smith's on the High Street. You should-a-seen the amazed looks those snooty girls gave us! We was paying cash—none of your 'on appro'! We bought orange hats, like we'd said, orange felt hats with a little bow at the back—we took our time, you bet we did!—and grey coats, exactly the same. The shoes— well, Sis didn't have them quite as high as me—we got them from Brum, we went there special.

We was all set for Blackpool!

*

Blackpool! That word has a mysterious ring, hasn't it! '*Black*-pool!' The brewery always seemed to go there; every year our Ede and our Jess or Jim would be talking about Blackpool and the next trip or the trip they'd just been on. In our living room we had a wot-not, and there were easy a hundred little Goss china ornaments that the others had brought back with them from brewery trips. 'BLACKPOOL' or 'A PRESENT FROM BLACKPOOL'. They took some dusting!

I remember Ede saying once: 'I'm goin to break some o' these buggers. I'm fed up wi dustin em.'

She did. She used to break one or two, gradually, to get rid of them. Then our Mother caught her, gave her such a sock o' the earhole. But she went on doing it. That was Ede—not deterred. How many times had I lifted up those little ornaments—boots 'n' shoes, dogs 'n' urns, you name it, we'd got it—read the letters out aloud: 'BLACK-POOL!' One was bigger than the rest: a china shell. You were s'pposed, when you put it to your ear, you were s'pposed to hear something. When I was a baby, then when I was a child, Else and Ede used to say: 'It's magic! It's the *sea* you can hear, the sea at *Black*-pool!'

Sis, Mary and 'chaperone' Doll on a brewery trip to Weston-super-Mare, 1930s: not the photograph referred to by Mary, which, tantalizingly, has vanished

Now I was grown, and I was going there for myself! It was the big treat. Every year the Flowers who owned the brewery had a 'do' at 'The Hill', like a garden party. They invited the workers up there: little sandwiches and that, a band, walk about the gardens. Sis and me went once, out of curiosity, but it wasn't what you'd call a *success*. We

didn't like to be watched, see, we didn't feel comfortable. The *trip*—
that *was* a treat!

We went by train, took all our own beer, loaded it up at the station.
It was a special train; every year they had it. Now that's a funny
thing, I can remember the train but I can't remember anything at all
about Blackpool! Only a photograph: there was me and Sis and Doll
Harben who was keeping an eye on us, walking along the Prom. I
don't know what happened to it. The wind was blowing. That's all
we did there, walk along the Prom; we didn't see the illuminations, or
the funfair, or the sea—it was the *train*!

A lot of the chaps and wenches had been drinking before we got
back to it—they were paralytic! But once aboard, nobody worried
you then! It was our very own train! Sis and me walked along the
corridors, up and down, up and down, you could say we *walked* back
to Stratford! Doll had lost interest in chaperoning.

'Ey, when did Doll disappear?'

'Miles an miles ago,' said Sis.

We shrieked! We thought we were very sophisticated. If we
spotted somebody we liked, somebody who was reasonably sober,
we went in. I didn't drink, nor did Harold Fogg.* He was a nice chap
and in the end I went and sat with him. The din! You could hardly
hear yourself think!

'You goin out with anyone special?' he said.

*

The older women didn't half tease me, Monday! They pulled my leg
'bout Harold. He phoned up.

'Your *chap's* on the line Mary!'

It was a blower thing; you called down for more beer. ''Ullo!' I
shouted. I loved using it.

Harold was in the cellars, but you could see he wasn't going to *stay*
there. He didn't lark about, Harold, like a lot of them did, he didn't
drink. He was a nice quiet sort o' chap, read books and that. He
didn't have a Dad, and his mother was quite old, nearer sixty 'n fifty.
He had three sisters. They all worked at the brewery; they were very
friendly, they were nice to me. They lived at the 'Eighteens' at
Wilmcote: a row of eighteen little stone cottages. I used to catch the
train and go there for tea, Sunday. Then Harold got a motorbike and
he used to pick me up on it, take me over there.

It was lovely! So peaceful—no rows, not like our house. After tea

* Pseudonym.

we went for walks, long walks on the Wilmcote moors. There were moors at Wilmcote, it was all gorse and rough land at the back of the Eighteens.

Our Mother trusted Harold, cos he was so nice; she never worried about me. She'd say: 'That lad's too nice for you, Mary Hewins!' I think that was why she was never strict with me, because she trusted him. She knew there was nothing to be strict *about*.

Chapter Five

Every Sunday night at our house we had card parties, for pennies and ha'pennies. Cyril organized them. All the young chaps came, and Dad kept a look out for the police. He'd be creeping upstairs, creep back, back'ards and for'ards, back'ards and for'ards, till our Mother shouted at him to stop, it was getting on her nerves.

I used to sit about and watch, look at one hand, then another. Jim slid one up his sleeve. You had to keep quiet . . . Arch Sweet was there, and Tom Holtom, Harry Wells and Fred Wells, Archie Smart, our Jim o'course and Brock Brookes, he was Jim's friend, a nice chap. He gave me two bob once. You know what two bob's like when you're fifteen! I don't know why he gave it to me—praps he'd had a big win.

' 'Ere y'are Mary—Mary Mary Quite Contrary!'

That's what they called me sometimes.

Anyway, I hid those two bob all over the place. I hid them under the oil cloth—we had oil cloth on our living room floor—nearly to the middle I got, you should a-seen me scrabbling away! I kept moving those two bob about, to be one step ahead of our Mother.

I thought: She won't find em 'ere!

You see, she'd never got any money. By Tuesday she was borrowing. She used to have Cyril's; Tuesdays she'd ask him if she could have her wages, what weren't due again till *Friday*! She'd be quite frightened to ask him—and *I* used to dread it! It was so regular! He ranted and raved, our Cyril, he grumbled so: 'What you *done* with it?' But the money was always there, in the end he always let her have it.

And Jim! He popped round on his bike dinner time and she said: 'Can I 'ave a couple o' bob?' He was married—he'd got married young, nineteen—but she asked him! She knew she could ask Jim and he wouldn't show off. He was the *giver*—and he was married, he'd got kiddies! Oh, our Jim, he used to let her do it. She knowed she could have anything she asked for, there. I felt so sorry for him, sometimes.

Always she was well in front of her wages; she could never catch up. 'Could I 'ave some money, Cyril, off me wages?' That's how it started; that was the warning sign. Or she sent me up to Mrs Windsor. Quick as I could without it being obvious, I went to my coat. I'd moved my two bob to the pocket of my top coat. My heart sank. She'd found it: there was nothing there! You never got it back.

Then Flo came to stay. She brought Ern—he was a Cockney, praps she'd met him when he came to do the gas, I don't know, Flo was very secretive, and their baby Teddy and Ern's brother Fred. He was only a young lad, ten or eleven, but so hungry!

'That lad could eat a horse!' our Mother said.

I thought: 'E very nearly 'as!'

I always dreaded them coming, so did Jess, though she never said anything, not like me. Jess was so quiet, 'put on'. I think that's what got on Dad's nerves. She took it all laying down, and her voice when she did speak was so low you'd a-thought she was apologizing for *having* a mouth.

'Speak up!' Dad shouted. 'Why don't you speak up?'

Straight from the brewery she went with me to clean the school, then half past six we came home and did the housework. I hung back a bit, got out of as much as I could. I was a little devil in those days. It was slabs in our kitchen; Jess scrubbed them when she got in, that was her first job, every night. Flo and Ern and Fred had been out somewhere, visiting. In they came, and the pram.

Jess said: 'Oh I've only just done that, Flo!'

Only a murmur, but just her luck, Dad heard! 'Bring it in!' he shouted, '*right* in! Don't take no notice of *er*!'

Jess was nearly in tears. The state of that floor, what with their muddy shoes, and the pram! They were all unfair to her: Flo, Dad, everybody. I was. Poor Jess! She brought out the worst in people; she never meant to, but she did. She was always the odd one out. She had a nice face, Jess, nice features and hair; only thing was, she'd got a mottled skin, as if she'd had smallpox. It spoilt her. She must have had smallpox as a child. It didn't seem fair.

She was the one who had *accidents*. You know, she went to the Mop, it was Sat'day night, packed o' course. You had to queue up for rides on the Big Horses and *then* they didn't stop proper at the end, to save time. Everybody was acting about but it was Jess who lost her balance when she tried to get off. The horse's head, its ears, came up and caught her here, on the breast.

We brought her home covered in bruises, sobbing. You never seen such a sight.

'They're *ruined!*' she said, over and over again, meaning her tits. Well, they were. Our Mother gave her some stout, made her drink it, cos she didn't like the taste.

'It'll fade, Jess,' I said, 'give it time.'

The funny thing was, she was a lot older'n me, but you always wanted to protect her, even if you did take advantage. Like when Flo and Ern and Fred came in with the pram I thought: So long as *I* don't 'ave to do that bloomin floor, now. Poor Jess!

*

Every summer they came like the swallows for their summer holidays: it was a good roost! Where did they sleep? I don't ever remember them sleeping—I only remember them *eating!* We'd got to feed them, and go to the shops to strap the food. Mostly it was me had to do it. It was a little shop in Brum Road, the strap shop, end of that terrace. I used to be frightened of going in. It was a horrible feeling, cos I *knowed* our Mother wouldn't pay. I was trembling, wondering what the man would say.

'Mam says, "Can we 'ave it . . ."'

He looked a bit desperate and all. Oh, if only the floor could a-swallowed me up!

'Er says, "Only for this week Mister Hirons."'

'You ain't paid for the week *before!*'

In the end he let us have it. Well, it was his living, I suppose, if you can call it that. Then I had to go somewhere else, for the next week or two.

One day towards the end of their holiday Flo said: 'I could do wi a bit o' money, to go back to London with.'

Jess and me looked at each other!

'I'll go peapickin—with our Mary.'

Peapicking weren't too bad, better than potato picking. That was hard! I'd been potato picking once with Ede. She went regular; she had to, to make her money up, her Tom didn't have much of a job. In bad weather he was out o' work. And our Else, she went once and all, I remember, cos her legs swelled up like an elephant's. Potato picking was terrible. They fetched you in an open lorry. Our Ede had to come and help me do my drift. I couldn't pick them up quick enough, see;

the tractor seemed to go so fast. They'd do it for spite, some of those drivers. Oh it was dreadful, backbreaking. Ede helped me to pick up, else I'd a-been too far behind.

Peapicking was easier, you could go at your own pace, put stones in the bottom of the sack. I couldn't say 'No' to our Flo. We walked up to the farm. The foreman was giving out the sacks and bawling: 'If you don't pick you don't earn!'
We knowed him well.
'Ullo,' he said, 'ow's Buckingham Palace?'
Flo pretended she hadn't heard.
'Ey that were a scrap and a 'alf your Jim was in Sat'day night, weren't it?'
The first thing I seen in the field was *gypsies*: lots of them! There was no turning back.
I said to Flo: 'Us'll go up far end.'
But when we came to have our peas weighed—a shilling a pot, 'bout that—it seemed the foreman had let one of these gypsies have a *pram* and she hadn't paid for it. He stopped her money. Ooh! That's when it started—in the barn. It was ugly. I can see this gypsy woman now, with plaits, twisted up like ram's horns.
She stood back and she laid a curse on him: 'Mark my words Mister, you'll be dead and in your coffin afore twelve months is out!'
He laughed! He just laughed. He said he'd got his money: he didn't care! But our Flo panicked! She ran! I had to run with her, over the fields. A storm was brewing. We dropped all the peas we'd pinched. I was more cross with Flo than frit—that surprised me. It was such a tradition in our family that I was scared of gypsies. It started to rain and then our Flo thought it might lighten. 'Ooh!'
'Come on Flo, let's shelter!' It was pouring.
She started counting. 'It'll *thunder* now!' She was terrified. 'Y'*see*!'
Stratford was below us, and the river. You could see the Parish Church and the river, like a scar, silvery white, fading. It was all fading, turning invisible, gone.
We ran across the fields in the blinding rain and we came home. It weren't till we was stripping by the fire I cried: 'Bloody 'ell! I never picked me money up!'
'I did,' said Flo.

Ern went back to London in advance. But that didn't make much difference; three could eat as much as four. When it was her turn to go our Flo started to cry. She was always one to cry when she went back. She cried and cried. All I could think of was: No more strap!

Our Mother said: 'You gotta go back to your 'usband!'

'Yes.' I said. It just came out.

Flo turned on me: 'What's it gotta do wi you?' She said: 'I know! Our Mary can go!'

There was me, hanging out the flags, and there was Flo in floods of tears! That was the unfairest thing of all, cos although she was so pretty, she was prettier'n any of us, with dark hair that waved on its own, big blue eyes, she was the cleverest too, our Flo.

Chapter Six

You know how you can get fancies? Your nose is too short or too long; if only you had hands like that, or longer lashes, something impossible. I hated my hair. It was dead straight, black; besides, bobs were out. Sis had lovely hair, wavy and fair, like Mary Pickford. They called me Anna May Wong—she was a Chinese film star—*Wonger* for short. 'SHE LURES MEN TO THEIR DEATH!' Permanent waves had just come in. I thought: '*That's* summat that ain't impossible!'

I saved up and I went to Inglis's on Henley Street and had a *perm*!

Well, it went all fluffy! Fluffy weren't so bad, but then it went frizzy! I looked such a sight!

I wailed: 'I look like a golliwog, Mam!'

Our Mother was picking through my hair; she always did it every morning, before I went to the brewery. I could tell what she was thinking: I *told you so*!

'It's 'orrible! I'm a freak! What's Sis goin to say?'

I knew Harold would say: 'You look lovely,' even if I'd got no teeth in. But Sis! I dreaded her opinion.

You had to check your hair every day, working at the brewery, cos some of them were so scruffy. There was one woman there, Agnes, she was definitely lousy. You could see them. When she combed her hair I always thought: Oh God! Can they jump? If she flirts one with that comb . . . If she was in the messroom, and I'd gone down to change into my clogs, if she was in the toilet, even if I was bursting I'd come out, quick.

All of a sudden our Mother shouts: '*Nits!*' She said: 'And you've been to the bloody hairdresser 'n' all! They must 'ave seen em!'

Oh no! I thought: She'll never get em out! It was so curly! I'll be late!

She had a job—scratch, scratch scratch with a black toothcomb—but she did it! She got every one out, she got the last nasty little bloodsucking nit out, cracked its back with her nail.

'When you're at brewery,' she said, low—I thought she was going to say 'Watch out for that Agnes,' but she said: 'D'ye notice Jess?'

'*Notice* er?'

'What er's like? Ow er *is*?'

'I dunno, Mam.'

I never gave our Jess a thought; I'd got better things to do.

'Ede says er's a-coughin.'

Well, Jess did cough. I thought: What's she gettin at? Jess used to annoy me cos when I smoked, sometimes I smoked in bed—'course, I slept with her—and she used to cry and tell our Mother the smoke got down her. I thought: She's been goin on again 'bout me smokin!

'Oh never mind,' said our Mother. 'Now you watch out for that Agnes—'

*

Jess had a trunk she kept her prizes in. She went to a lot of whist drives at the Hippodrome and she was always winning. That was the one thing she was lucky at. I loved to go through this chest with her, look at them: a complete set of cutlery, a mantel clock, beautiful stuff. One night she came back with a box that big.

'What you got, Jess?'

She was excited, pale—well, she always was—but this day she looked really happy.

'It's a *lemonade set*!'

I'd never heard of one of those. It was beautiful: a jug and six green glasses, magical, each one different but the same.

'They're hand made' she said, 'see the bubbles.'

'They're *lovely*, Jess.'

There were tiny bubbles in the glass. When you held one up to the light it was like the river, you know, if you put your head under, swimming.

'Won't e be pleased!'

'Oo?'

'Frank.'

'Oh *im*.'

She was building up her bottom drawer. Well, she was going out with Frank Pollitt;* she'd went with him a long time. I didn't like him, but you couldn't tell Jess. She was nicer'n any of us, she never saw the dark side o'folks.

Then she had this terrible row with Dad—or *he* had one with her.

* Pseudonym.

She never argued back. She just bit her lip and bowed her head and that seemed to make him more infuriated—or started coughing. She couldn't get her breath; she coughed and coughed and coughed. And she'd stopped eating.

At first it just seemed to irritate Dad, but when she got thinner and thinner then he got angry, 'specially Sunday dinner time when he came back from the pub, half past one, two o'clock.

'Eat it!' He was up the pole: not rolling drunk, just argumentative.

'I *can't!*' said Jess.

'I'll show you if you can or can't.' And he chucked her dinner up the fire! Sometimes he chucked his and all—the whole table! *I* was alright, well I'd always ate mine—*fast*—before he got back.

The more Jess didn't eat or argue or do anything the more wild it made him.

'Where you goin?'

'I'm meetin Frank.'

'Not that bleedin Frank Pollitt?'

Our Mother used to come between them, and o' course I always stuck up for her, cos I was on her side, always. I couldn't abide Dad, 'specially when he was drunk.

'Let er go, George!'

'She oughta see a *doctor*. That's oo she should be seein.'

'She 'as.' That shook Dad. 'E says it's a touch o' bronchitis.'

'*Bronchitis!*' Dad cussed and raved. He thumped on the table and shouted at Jess: 'Do you *want* to die?'

Well, this day there was an argument and a half. Jess snook out, but Dad wouldn't let up; even after she'd gone he was carrying on about how she should eat and where was her spirit and fancy taking up with a bastard like Frank Pollitt.

Our Mother never tried to stop him when he got into one of his rages. She just let him go on. He never hit her, or tried to; he never hit any of us. *She* used to do the hitting! Hit you round the head, she did, but not Dad—never. That was one thing about him, he never did that. No, it was *words*—terrible. He was a real devil with *words*, Dad. As for our Mother, she never cried, she just got in a flaming temper.

It was all the time, the rows in our house, practically all the time. This day—well, it was night cos the row had been going on since dinner time, on and off—Cyril joined in, and then it was three against one.

Suddenly Dad shouts: '*Out!*'

We stared.

'Both o' you! *Get out!*'

I realized he meant me and Cyril! We were so astonished—we *did*! We got outside; it was dark, we didn't know where to go. The only person we could think of was our Jim. We thought: That's where we'll go!

It was a hell of a walk to Wilmcote. I'll never forget it: all that way! It was August, lucky for us, not too cold, but I had high heels on. I was more dead 'n alive by the time we got there, past midnight. Jim and his wife lived in the Number Tens; the Eighteens where the Foggs lived was up the road. If Harold could see me now! We started throwing stones to knock Jim up.

His head poked out. 'What the hell?'

When we told him he said: 'I'll come back with you—now! Sort the ole bugger out!'

'I can't, Jim! I can't walk back in these!'

Jim was wild. He was going to fight our Dad, he said. We'd be better off without him; we were better off when he was away in the war. I 'spect we was, but I couldn't remember.

'Pity e ever came back! Mam found a letter, y'know, from a woman.'

I did know, cos Else had told me.

'It made er cry.'

That shocked me; I'd never seen her cry.

'She's 'ad a rotten life, our Mother.'

He seemed to have forgot 'bout Cyril and me—and Jess.

*

After that night, you can imagine, Jess panicked. Well she'd been the cause of it, really. She thought Dad would throw *her* out. She started to pack all her prizes up. In the rush she broke two of the glasses. She wasn't half upset, crying and sobbing. 'The jug's cracked 'n' all!'

'Never mind,' I said, 'they was too delicate, really.'

'It's spoilt,' she said, 'the set's spoilt!'

'What you doin it for, Jess? All this packin? Where'll you *go*?'

It was bad enough her coughing all night and going on about me smoking, and tossing and turning—but *sobbing*!

She made me promise not to tell Dad, or Cyril, or Bert.

'I'm sendin em to Frank,' she said, 'for safe keepin. There's a railway wagon comin round in the mornin. Don't you breathe a word our Mary, *promise*!'

She made me swear I wouldn't tell.

34

I thought, No chap's worth this, and 'specially *im*. But I kept my thoughts private.

*

I was proved right. As soon as he knew, Frank Pollitt, soon as he knew she'd got it, he gave her up. And he kept all those lovely things: all except the four green glasses, cos the set was spoilt so she hadn't put them in. She was broken-hearted. She'd been going with him three years, but he never came round again, when he heard she'd got TB.

She left the brewery. She did the school for a bit longer—all that dust!—but in the end she didn't go outside any more. Then the day came when she didn't come downstairs; she stayed abed. Her back was all hunched, her bones sticking out of her skin.

I heard the doctor say: 'It's the best solution, Mrs Hewins . . . oo wears them shoes?' He'd spotted my shoes by the bed!

'My youngest.'

'Tell er she'll be a cripple afore she's thirty.'

Our Mother said, low, cos Jess was there, I had to strain my ears: 'She ain't a-goin!'

'If she don't t'other un'll get it, bound to, sleepin with er—everybody—the boy—'

I think that's what made our Mother agree for Jess to go to Hertford Hill. Bert had never been fit, well, ever since a babby he'd been sickly. He had a cough, always had a dry cough. But about this time he started, you know, to blossom. I remember seeing him riding Bomber's horse back to the field and getting quite a shock: he was laughing, little rosy cheeks. Jess was dying and he was starting to bloom. A flower on a rubbish heap, that's what life is like.

Chapter Seven

There were no letters from Hertford Hill. We all knew that was a bad sign.

'Floods or no floods,' said our Mother, 'I'm a-goin.'

'You won't get through, river's right up,' said Dad, 'water's this deep, bottom of town! Swan's Nest's marooned!'

'What's swans' nests got to do with it?' You could see her mind was made up.

I said: 'Harold'll take me Sat'day, Mam, on 'is motorbike. E can try back way.'

Nothing we could say would budge her. She stuck her hatpin through her hat. It was only an ordinary little movement, I seen her doing it every day of my life, but even now, remembering, it stabs my heart. She put her coat on, then her hat, with a hatpin—without looking. There was a whiff of Cologne. It was like reaching for a gun, the way that hat went on and the pin went in, a similar sort of movement. You knew she meant business.

Watching her, I was a kiddie again; she was big, and I was small. She never walked very fast. We'd get outside and her hand reached down—a precise movement. When her hand came down you didn't hesitate: your hand was there, waiting for hers. It was a firm grip. You felt confident she would get anything she wanted, from the shops, the market, anywhere. When she said she'd get through the floods you didn't argue.

Hours later she came back, soaked to the skin, drenched.

'Bloody bus driver!'

That's all she'd say. She poked the coal till I thought: God, er's goin to set chimney on fire! I could see Dad thinking the same. But it was more than his life was worth to douse it; he daren't, with her in that sort o' mood. 'Bloody man!'

'I'll get Harold to take me tonight,' I said.

So I went. Harold took me to the bottom of the hill and waited. E's a nice chap! I thought. 'Too nice for *you*, Mary Hewins!' the echo said, 'too nice!' It was the worst springtime in living memory, so you can picture the weather, and getting dark and all. When I got past the trees a terrible sight met my eyes: the shadows of hundreds of little huts, on the hill, some with lights flickering, most of them black and *dead* looking. I told myself: Just don't think 'bout it! I kept climbing and climbing. It was like a dream—a nightmare.

King Edward VII Memorial Chest Hospital, Hertford Hill, near Warwick

'Er'll be at the top,' they'd said at the gate, 'in cowsheds.'
That's what they'd called them.
I was climbing all the time. I was past being frit. Harold had said he'd come with me, but I knowed our Jess. She wouldn't a-wanted anyone 'cept us. I found her, God knows how. It *was* a hut, right at the very top, and all open. They'd each got a little wooden hut, 'bout the size of a garden shed. There was no door, no glass in the windows; the wind and the rain blowed through.
'Oh Jess,' I said. You could see why she hadn't writ; she was too weak for anything. She didn't even want to talk. I looked at her and I thought: She's got no life. She was skin 'n' bones, she just lay there.
There was a plate of cold taters on the side, with a number on it—number fourteen—and some gravy. You could see she hadn't

touched it. I felt I'd got to try to feed her. If she eats summat, that might save her! All of a sudden I thought: That's why Dad used to get in such a rage! I tried her with a bit of apple. I'd brought a bag of apples, saved from the autumn. We scrumped them from Schofield's orchard: keepers, with a bitter skin. I never knew their name. They weren't much cop now, cidery, wizened, but I thought maybe the smell of them . . . It was no good. She was pleased to see me, I could tell from her eyes, her eyes was open, all the time, but she wouldn't eat. She didn't even cough. There was a pot to spit in: that had number fourteen on it too. I went on peeling apples, the whole bloody lot, one after the other. Number fourteen—what did that mean? Well, it was the only thing I could think of to *do*, trying to feed her, and talk. I talked and talked and talked, about what was going on at home, and our Mother and Dad. She always wanted to be *family*, Jess, not like me; she clung to the family.

I began. I said: 'There was a big row at our 'ouse, Monday mornin. A real scream 'n' shout.'

That got her smiling, well, the shadow of a smile. *That* was just like home!

'You know ow I lets Mam or you answer the door?'

I always did, in case it was gypsies. You see, when I was little our Mother would say: 'If you don't do what you're told the gypsies'll 'ave you. They brought you, they'll take you back!' All of them used to say I was brought by the gypsies, I don't know why. Maybe it was on account of my hair—as I said, it was black, straight as pump water—I don't know. 'If you don't be'ave, our Mary, gypsies can 'ave you back!'

Well, Sunday night there was a hammering on our door and I said to myself: 'It's Arch 'n' Norman come for cards!' I never *thought*! I opened the door—and there stood the ugliest and blackest woman you ever seen! Like a tramp, with an old shawl over her head—horrible. I wanted to say: 'Bugger off!' but she'd struck me dumb, just the *sight* of her.

'I come for George.'

'Oo is it?'

I never answered our Mother; I couldn't! That brought her to the door. Even she was took aback.

'What d'ye want?'

There was summat mysterious 'bout that cock-eyed Irish woman; for a start, she hadn't got a basket, nor kiddies. 'I come for George, missus.' She was quite polite. 'I tried the Dragon but e ain't there.'

You should a-seen the look our Mother gave her! 'E ain't 'ere neither. What d'ye want?' She wouldn't let her over the step. 'Never let em over the step' was her motto.

'I've summat for im.' She brought out a little package. It looked like a half-crown, wrapped in a mucky bit o' brown paper. Our Mother took it, quick, she almost snatched it! Well, generally it was the other way round: our Dad giving money away!

'I'll see e gets it.' She said to me: 'Go'n cut a slice off that puddin in the kitchen. *I'll stop 'ere.*'

I cut a big slice, bigger'n I meant to, I was that nervous. There goes my dinner tomorrow, I thought—well, the best bit of it.

'The Lord bless you, missus,' said the cock-eyed Irish woman.

Our Mother slammed that door! She put the bolt across! She wasn't half in a temper.

'Not that er don't owe it us!' she said, ' 'alf County Cork owes us money! It's 'avin to take it!' and: 'I wonder where the bugger is?'

I watched the woman from our window. When she got down the road a few yards—do you know what she done? She throwed that pudding away! As far as it would go. It landed in the Wells's front garden.

'Well,' our Mother was saying, '*well!*'

It wasn't money, after all, it was a silver badge. I saw: 'FOR SERVICES RENDERED'.

'Well,' I said—Jess was still listening, her eyes never left me, 'our Dad wasn't 'alf upset!'

For a start, he got locked out. I had to creep downstairs and let him in. And then the badge: that seemed to upset him. But missing that cock-eyed Irish woman upset him most of all. Next morning he was still on about it: 'Did she 'ave one blue eye and one *brown*, our Mary?'

'I dunno.' I wished he'd shut up; it would only get our Mother going.

'Which way did she go, our Mary?'

'I dunno.' It was true; I never seen.

'Brummagem way? Was she headin to'ards Brummagem?'

'She was headin to'ards Devil's country by the looks on er,' said our Mother. 'I never seen a more evil looking personage, in all my born days. 'Cept your Gran, o'course.'

Then they rowed! You can imagine! His Gran had brought him up, you see. They were still rowing when the brewery hooter went. That was me off, like Cinderella, only glad to be out of it! I didn't leave a slipper behind! No fear! I dreaded coming home, but when I did—there was our Mother polishing up that silver badge, as sweet as pie. 'It'll come in for the *next* time your Dad meets the Prince! If we can keep im sober!'

I looked at Jess. I thought: I can't stop now! I said: 'You heard 'bout the Prince o' Wales openin the new Theatre,* didn't you?'

I gave her a running account of everything that had happened in our family, every little thing. And when I went, I felt I was helping to kill her, going. But I was glad to get out. I can't describe it; it was like being *with* death. I had to escape! When I got out I ran down that hill—it was pitch black—high heels and all. I couldn't get away fast enough. When I fell down all I thought was: I'm still alive!

*

So I wasn't surprised when our Mother said about the guinea-pigs.

The river was down. She'd went on the bus to Hertford Hill, well to Warwick, they would only take you as far as Warwick. She'd walked miles and miles along that road to Hertford Hill. The buses never went up there—no fear!

'I seen em,' she said, 'like furry rats.' She'd been on about the guinea-pigs ever since she got back. She couldn't get them out of her mind. They was on mine and all now! And Dad's! 'Like furry rats,' she said, 'only fatter.'

'I'm off,' said Dad.

I thought: I don't blame you!

'They shown me. They said: "We inject em from the patients. This is er un. We inject from the patients and if one of em dies . . ."'

She didn't say Jess's guinea-pig had died; she didn't have to. But what she said next did surprise me: 'She's comin 'ome.'

She had our George's old room. Bert and Cyril came out, slept with me. She had to have a room on her own. Poor Jess, even at home she had to be alone. As for Bert, well he wasn't upset; he didn't know what was happening. Jess had never had much to do with him, really; she'd been at work all the time. Our Mother had brought him up. He didn't understand. He was only nine.

I never sat with her; our Mother wouldn't let me.

'You gotta go to work in the mornin,' she said.

I think she was frit I might catch it. Mostly she sat with her, and Jim's wife, and Dad.

* The new Shakespeare Memorial Theatre was opened on 23 April 1932.

On the seventh day she said: 'Fetch Vicar, George, don't argue,' and to me: 'Get er good nightgown out,' and: 'It was the Big Horses at the Mop. I knows it was the Big Horses.'

I didn't say anything. Our Ede reckoned it was the brewery killed her. In the early days they'd had to stand in water, up to here, and no daylight. But our Mother wouldn't have that. She didn't want to hear, so I didn't say anything. I tried to sew a button on. My fingers were trembling. I remember I couldn't thread the needle.

Dad was with her when she died. I can see him now, when she died, cos I ran in, I heard this *sound*. He'd pulled the pillow from under her head; he was hurling it against the floor. He bashed it on the floor. You never seen such a mess! Feathers everywhere. It was snowing feathers. Jess just lay there, silent, dead, but out of his throat was coming this horrible sound, like a wild creature being throttled.

Four men pulled the bier from Park Road. We walked behind. All the neighbours were out. Mrs Wells, she was in her front, she shouted: 'It's no bloody good *now*, George, you should a-looked after er when she was alive!'

Sis came with me; she was crying ever so.

Flo wrote from London: 'I want to remember my sister as she was.'

Our Mother said: 'Flo's too upset to come.'

I could picture Jess smiling, you know, how we used to share a smile over Flo, just the shadow of one, but a smile. Oh Jess! I thought, I'm going to miss you.

We followed her all the way from Park Road to the church, and from the church to the cemetery.

Our Mother said, 'Ow funny,' she said, 'there's Sis—' Sis Crowe was Jess's only friend, she'd died twelve months before. I think a chap had chucked her up and it broke her heart.

'And ole Mister Beard off the road—'

She knew where they all were, under the grass.

'And er.'

A stranger came round; we were examined, everybody. And the bedding was burnt, in the garden: her mattress, the sheets, her clothes, everything. Poor Jess, there wasn't a trace of her left, 'cept those four green glasses—and Bert. She was so quiet, she was the best of us all. She'd never had any life.

'I can't abide this house,' said Dad.

For once, there was no argument.

Chapter Eight

The School House, Alcester Road, Stratford-upon-Avon (1983)

That's why the school house seemed so magical. When Dad came home and said: 'School house is vacant. The new headmistress don't want to live there', we didn't think much about it. What was the point? But when he said: 'There's a chance for *us*! If I gets round Vicar there's a chance!' and 'Ow about it?' it seemed as if, you know, we'd each had a wish and it had been granted. 'We'll 'ave to go to Communion, Sunday,' Dad said. He'd got a plan. 'Course, he asked our Mother first, everybody did that. She said 'yes' or 'no'. But there was no need, hardly. Her face! The *school house*!

She chucked everything out. The wot-not went, the fancy cushions from the rummage, the photo of Dad in his Volunteer's uniform, all the Theatre ladies hanging along the wall with their signatures, signed to her, signed specially to her because she'd used to dress them. '*To Emma, with love*', '*Dearest Emma from Violet Farebrother*'. All those beautiful things went crashing into the bin, one after the other, all gone 'cept the china shell. That survived, somehow—I remember seeing it later—and Dad's certificate. When I was little I used to lay there and read it and read it: '1917—*Discharged*—George Henry Hewins—Royal Warwickshire Regiment—*Honourably* Discharged —1917.' Somebody had signed it for him: '*George*'. I rescued that. I rolled the certificate up and I kept it. God knows why.

'It's a new start!' she said. She was whipped up with excitement. Her eyes shone. Her hair started to come back: she'd lost it in great handfuls, after Jess died. Rip-rip, bang-bang, smash-smash. Dad let her get on with it. Well, it would a-been like trying to stop a March wind. We all have our own ways of grieving.

'Just look at that larder! Fancy!'

It was a lovely larder, ever so big, with shelves all round, red tiles on the floor.

'Like larder at "Shakespeare",' she said.

She couldn't get over it.

'And a cellar! Just think what us'll be able to keep down there!'

I thought: 'Alf the brewery, if I knows our———

'*Look*!'

We went from room to room and she was flushed with happiness. Then we went outside. There was a high wall round the back garden so's nobody could see us; the playground was over the wall. One side was dirt, and a few flowers.

'We can keep hens, still,' she said. 'That's where I'll 'ave the hen run.'

For her the school house was a dream come true. It stood on its own, beside the school, separate yet *part* of it, with stone-faced windows, some with diamonds. There was a porch and a front door with four arch shaped panes—like a church! Wonderful! She kept going in and out of that door, in and out.

'Well,' she said, '*well*!' and 'This porch'll come up lovely with sand!'

Dad never said what put the new headmistress off. But he always kept a bottle on the front window sill, with '*RAT POISON*' on it, in big letters.

You'd a-thought *I'd* have been in seventh heaven too. At last I'd got our Mother to myself—with the Dragon just opposite Dad was out permanently and our Cyril had got just as bad—that's what I'd always wanted. But it wasn't enough. I was restless. I loved her, but you can't explain feelings. They're like the river; you can feel it pulling you always, pulling you away from the bathing place, pulling you where you don't want to go, where you know it's dangerous.

*

'This young gentleman's startin today and I'll be obliged if one of you older uns ud show im the ropes.'

'It'll be a *pleasure*, Mister Court!' All the women laughed.

'The bottling end', Flowers Brewery, Stratford-upon-Avon, late 1930s

I pitied the young lads, starting. You see, they didn't know what was in store for them. It was like lambs to the slaughter. When a new lad started at the bottling end, the women—the older women— would be waiting . . . They'd have a laugh, get him on the floor— well, you can picture it—get a bottle of Guinness or a Number One Strong Ale, that was a long narrow bottle, shook it up a bit. It was *potent*, not the bottle, the ale, and it started to fizz and he'd shout '*Ow!*'

I used to dread it. I kept out of it if I could, went outside to the heap or down to the messroom.

'Come on, Sis. Let's tek this lot to heap.' This day I hadn't realized there was a new one starting. There he was, before I could escape.

It was *him*! The boy on the bicycle! I couldn't believe it! What was he doing at the brewery? There was no mistaking!

'Ey Ginger!' one of the women shouted. 'You ginger *all over*?'

'There's only one way to find out!'

He *wasn't* ginger; he was auburn. His hair was like dark copper. Well—he stood there and he grinned! He grinned and he gave them such a look—not nasty, but . . . it shut them up.

I thought: Oh God, e's goin to pay for this, later! I had the wild idea of warning him. What was he doing at the brewery? He must be in the office! But he wasn't! He was only unloading the wagons when the empties came in, he was only doing a labouring job. What was a grammar school boy doing *labouring*? I thought: E's goin to be for it!

Lucky for him there was a commotion that morning, took their minds off everything else. Sis fell in the glass heap.

I went to the hospital to see her. She wasn't half in a mess, covered with bits o' glass. We used to have to take crates o' glass bottles that had broke to the heap, you see; two of us had to carry them. It was like a slag heap, like they have at pit heads: just a great big sparkling heap of glass. They'd got nowhere else to put it; nobody wanted broken glass. Well, I was dreaming, Sis tripped and fell right in! There was bits o' glass splinters everywhere, all over her hands and her legs and her back. She was in tears still.

'They 'ad to pick em out wi tweezers! They ain't done *yet*! Look!'

'S'not on your face, Sis. That's one good thing,' I said. 'Ey, you know that lad oo started today? Do you remember im?'

She didn't.

'On 'is bike! The boy on the bicycle!'

She didn't remember! I was glad, somehow.

'I seen im once at Wilmcote. I reckon e lives near Wilmcote.'

I'd seen his bike when I'd been out walking with Harold, propped against a wall. It was so distinctive—like him. Poor Sis! I was more interested in solving the mystery than sympathizing with her, and she wouldn't a-gone to the heap in the first place if it hadn't been for me.

*

Next day in the messroom—I had to take beer down there for a

45

couple of the women—I was straining my ears. They never mentioned him. They were still debating whether Sis's beauty had been spoilt forever—*hopin*, I thought. One of them, she only had one eye; a bottle had bust and took the other out. She used to start on Guinness before breakfast; six o'clock she was usually drunk, by breakfast she was up the pole. Jack Timms the foreman was on to those who drank. The women weren't allowed beer, not like the men, so they got one of us young ones as didn't drink to take bottles down to the messroom.

'I've gotta go to toilet again, Mister Timms!'

One of the Mattock* girls kept a couple back in her knickers, went out with them at night and her elastic broke—half way down Windsor Street! In the middle of the pavement!

I was just going back up the steps when I heard a woman say: 'Did you see? Ow that ginger lad looked at Sal yesterday?'

'Took the wind out er sails!'

'You know oo e *is*?'

'Poor lad!'

'You'll console im I s'ppose?'

They laughed.

I daren't stop no longer. I'd had to get somebody to take my place. Besides, the foreman knew everything that went on, and Gargy Court the manager, he had an office right up in the ceiling so's he could get a bird's eye view. He watched you pull your stockings up. When you went downstairs he timed you. He didn't dock it, but he'd call Jack Timms and get him to tell you off if you stopped a long time.

*

When Sis was better, her and her chap and me and Harold went to the pictures, in the good seats. We lashed out; well, Harold paid. Sis said after: 'Did you see that lovely brooch?'

'Ey?'

'That lovely brooch er was wearin. You know, in the farewell scene.'

I hadn't. Sis laughed. 'What was you two doin?'

We hadn't been doing *any*thing. And I'd got a blooming awful headache. I felt my head was going to drop off. Another few steps, I thought, and it will. I didn't tell Harold—I couldn't a-stood the fuss—nor Sis. But when I got home I told our Mother.

'You'd best go to doctor,' she said.

* Pseudonym.

46

So I did. I went to the surgery on Rother Street.

'Please I've got bad headaches!'

I was frit to death; I'd never been to a doctor before! I didn't know what to say, what you were supposed to *do*. So imagine my face when Dr Pembrey smiled and said: 'We'll go down the cellar.'

He lifted a trapdoor in the floor and I thought: It must be a dream! It can't be happening! There were plenty of people waiting—I could a-screamed and been rescued—but I was too frit! I saw stone steps, going down.

'Follow me,' he said.

Now if there's one thing I can't abide it's a cellar. I never could share our Mother's pleasure in the cellar at the school. They are dreadful places.

'Come on,' he said, 's'alright.'

How I managed it I do not know. It was pitch black. We'd only gone a few steps and he said: '*Stop!*'

He shone a torch into my eyes.

'Hrumphhh!'

I thought: E's goin to murder me!

'It's very bad,' he said, 'did nobody ever test your eyes at *school*? Ow've you managed?'

I was struck dumb. He sounded so angry! I thought he was blaming *me*. But my brain was racing. That's why I couldn't follow the film proper! *Any* film! Or thread needles. Or read, or tell the time! That's why I'd always gone by colours more'n faces, how somebody smelt, sounded, the touch of things more'n the look. I couldn't *see*!

' 'Ave you any money?' he said. His voice was quite kind. 'You'll need 'bout two pound.'

Our Mother said: 'Us'll get it.'

Two pounds was Dad's weekly wages. I knowed Mrs Windsor wouldn't have that sort o' money to lend, nor our Cyril, nor anybody at short notice. Well, to cut a long story short, everybody clubbed in, our Jim and all.

'Ask no questions!' he said.

That was one thing about our family, they would help you if they could, no strings attached.

I got the two pound and I went to the opticians. He was an old man—well, I'll tell you straight, he was a dirty old man. He took me into a little dark room, he was awful. When I went for my fitting—

'It's your fittin, innit?' leer-leer—he touched me like this. Ugh! I was glad to get out—glad till I remembered what I'd paid those two pounds for: *glasses*!

I didn't want to wear them, I didn't want to *see* myself. I avoided looking in the shop windows. I didn't like them a bit. 'Course, Harold said they suited me! How could glasses *suit* you? Everybody stared at work. Well, not many people like us wore glasses then, it was toffs did, mostly: I was the only girl in the brewery with them. Horrifying things.

'Ooh!' they said, 'Mary's got glasses!' and: 'Ow does it feel to 'ave four eyes, Mary?'

I thought: That's it! I've 'ad it now!

But I was determined to keep them on; that was my stubborn nature. Through that glass—it's hard to describe—the world was a different place, so bright, shining. I could see the tiles on the school roof and the bell, I could even see a bird on top of our chimney stack and know before it started squawking that it was an old crow, watching our Mother's chicks most likely, and the lime trees, and every single leaf and the sun turning the clouds . . . a shining, shining world.

Chapter Nine

I'd been laying elaborate plans how I could get to talk to him. Once I got those blooming glasses I thought: That's it! So picture my surprise when he comes up to me at work one day, cool as a cucumber, and says: 'Shall I give im a message?'

I was that took aback I was quite rude. 'Oo?'

'Harold o' course.'

'Oh.'

He knew I went out with Harold! He must a-seen me at Wilmcote, visiting the Foggs. Just my luck. He didn't say no more, well, he probably thought I was gormless the way I looked at him, stared. He went back to humping the crates. Once or twice after that in a quiet voice he asked about Harold; he had a quiet, deep sort of voice, but cheeky. Trouble was, I wanted him to be more'n just cheeky. I wanted him to mind, to be jealous . . . I'd go red with my own thoughts.

'Penny for em,' said Harold. He put something into my hand. 'It's a present,' he said, 'for the nicest girl in the world.'

I should a-said: 'And you're the nicest boy!' That was true! But I was too choked up. It's hard to explain, but even Harold *breathing* was an irritation to me. I could a-screamed. I opened the box and there was a wrist watch! None of us had wrist watches. It was lovely, with a square face, silvery coloured.

'It's the latest style.'

I knew. I'd seen them up the town. Sis and me had hung over them in the jeweller's window. It had cost a lot of money.

'It's not a cheap un.'

'Oo wants to know ow much it bloody cost?'

'I only thought—'

I heard myself say: 'It's 'orrible. I can't abear *silver*. Nor square watches. Nor oblong ones.'

Harold looked shocked, you know, as if he'd picked up a ferret by mistake.

''Ere,' I said, 'I don't wannit.' I thought: I'm doin you a favour, Harold Fogg. You're better off wi'out me.

He didn't argue. Who could blame him? He had his pride. Off he went, across the 'croft, squaring his shoulders up. I wished he'd a-said: 'You little bitch!' I wished he'd a-said something nasty. I thought of his old mother and his sisters waiting at home for him—'Did she like it, Harry?'—and for a moment there I weakened. I felt sorry, ashamed. But his future wasn't mine. It's something you know. We've all got our own star to follow.

*

He was my star; well he changed my life, you could definitely say *that*! When he said: 'You comin to the Mop tomorrer night?' I said 'Yes!' And I sang inside.

Collins's *Dragons*—that was the star attraction! They'd got the music, the organ! They were lovely; each dragon had red velvet seats. You ran your hand over it—soft, soft!—like thick moss, plush. Everyone was drunk, even I'd had a port and brandy. The dragons were magical. You chose one and you sat in it, you felt you were sailing through the clouds. They were my favourite. Every now and then they switched the lights off, the main lights, and it was *dark*! Everyone screamed! Round and round the dragons went, round and round, music blaring away and our skirts flew up.

He said, 'I shall 'ave to get off.'

Funny, but it was when he admitted . . . There was a feeling inside of me—happiness? I don't know. It was more ex*cite*ment. Tonight! Tonight! Some chaps you'll keep messing about for years . . .

A man was shouting: 'Tonight! The *Wall of Death*!'

We watched from the top.

'We're mad!' I said, 'ain't we mad payin to watch this?'

You could see he was fascinated. He felt it too now! The ex*cite*ment! They went faster and faster, those chaps on motorbikes, round and round they went—they'd rev up—faster and faster and faster. They got to the top, smothered in oil and stuff. I touched one of them—and jumped back! All the girls did it—'*Oooh!*' We thought that was wonderful.

When I cried out he caught hold of my arm. He was laughing at me.

'S'alright,' he said, 's'alright!'

'It's terrible,' I said. 'Ey, 'ave you ever *seen* a death on this thing?'
'No,' he said, 'I never.' He laughed!
'It's bloody marvellous ow they do it, though.'
'Let's go back to Cross Keys.'
'No,' I said, 'I can't stand chaps oo drink.'
'Nor me roundabouts.'
So we walked through Old Town. Most of the lights was off—it was late!—by the Parish Church there and over the bridge, till we'd left the Mop behind, and the music and the screams.

Chapter Ten

I snook out the bottling end and walked along the bridge, just to see him. Lots of times I did it. There was a wooden bridge, way up, like in the sky, over the Golden City. I used to walk along it, trying to catch his eye. If the foreman caught me I'd say:

'I got a message for our Jim!'

'The Golden City', Flowers Brewery, Stratford-upon-Avon

Once a year they cleaned the vats out, and all the chaps they'd strip down to the waist, well down to their underpants; some didn't wear nothing, just a strip o' cloth and canvas shoes. They went down the ladders and they cleaned the vats out with a sort of pumice stone. You could see the froth on the beer of those that were still full. Deep they were, deep as a house, and you know how beer stains! It was filthy work, hard, but as it came up, the copper, the whole place started to shine gold, you never seen anything so beautiful—and the chaps! They turned to gold, with the reflection.

I'd make him look up. The others laughed; I didn't care. He could stand on his own with them. He was well developed for his age, muscular, you'd never a-thought he weren't one of them. He worked alongside the other chaps, he could work as hard as our Jim or anybody. I used to think: He's mine! A golden prince in a golden city.

I must have been mad.

*

I hardly noticed Sis get married. We had a row; it was over a chap—it was over *him*. Well, she used to tease me 'bout him, say she'd been out with him, that sort o' thing. Then one day, on the spur of the moment almost, she got married! 'Course, we weren't speaking so I didn't get an invitation. It served me right; I'd started it. She married Syd, and afterwards she went to live at Coventry.

I've often wondered since: if Sis hadn't gone . . . She was my best friend; she was never frit of saying what she thought, and maybe . . . You never realize how you value something till you lose it, you know, like being careless with a necklace, and then you think: Oh if only I'd took good care of it! After the beads have scattered.

Missing Sis get married was very ironical cos I'd always loved a wedding; we both had. We'd never had one in our family, a good wedding: our George and Marg went to Leamington, on bikes, Flo did it in London and Jim went to the registry. Folks'd look in the photographer's window and say: 'Oo's she?' or: 'What's them two doin?' I got on everybody's photo. There I was on the shot of the bride and groom coming down the path, or with the relations by the gate. I didn't do it on purpose, it was just we couldn't keep away if we heard the bells, and we liked to get a good look.

We'd planned ours and all! We opened the *Herald* and it said: 'The bride, Miss Mary Hewins,' or 'Miss Emily Wells . . . wore a dress of parchment satin and carried a bouquet of red roses with a sprig of myrtle. The bridesmaids, Miss So 'n' So, cousin of the bride, and Miss Da de Da, friend of the bride, wore floral georgette and carried posies of sweet peas. The bridegroom's gift to the bride was a string of cultured pearls . . .'

Well, not long after Sis had gone, one of the girls at the brewery sent me an *invitation*! Lily wasn't a friend to go out with, more refined, she didn't swear or anything like Sis 'n' me; Hilda Mattock was her very best friend. She always appeared one above us. She had the nicest jobs at the brewery, you know, where it wasn't *dirty*, like putting the tops on the bottles—pleated, a little red cap, then you put a rubber ring round. That was a nice job. I 'spect Jack Timms . . . Anyway, Lily invited me to her wedding, so I went.

The reception was in the hut up Clopton Road. Afterwards *he* came to meet me. 'Course he hadn't been invited; he was different, wasn't one of us. They all said he was stuck up, and he drank too much and what could I see in him? *They'd* gone off him completely!

I ignored it. I thought: They're jealous.

He'd been drinking. This night up Clopton Road he was drunk as a lord.

I said: 'Poor Fred, e always wanted Lily. E wanted to marry er really. I think e'll 'ave Hilda now,' just to take my mind off it. He was being sick by the palings.

'*Why?*' I said, 'why do you *do* it?'

The sound of it sloshing out, the retching! I stood and watched him being sick all over the palings there—I'd got my new Marina dress on for Lily's wedding—and the pavement. The stink! Princess Marina had just come on the scene. It was a very pretty blue-green, Marina green they called it.

Oh God! I thought, I can't bear it!

There was a cape, with frills round, at the top, just a small one. It reminded me of Dad. And others.

I asked him: 'Why do you *do* it?' I said, 'You'll never catch up with them, no matter how hard you try.'

I shouldn't a-said that, probably. It was red rag to a bull. But I could see no sense in it, I didn't know what was driving him. *Some*thing was.

Why did I stop with him? It must have been his looks. It gets you, it gets you into trouble, it leads you into God knows where. There's nothing else, I thought, only his looks! He's wild, terrible wild. To have Councillor Smith tell him he was a disgrace! Yes, that's what he'd said! He told me, laughing.

'You *are*!' I said.

But I loved him. There's no accounting for it; I'm not asking anyone else to understand. Why should they? He was one on his own, he was unique.

Then the most amazing thing happened: our Mother had a win on the Pools! Not much—but it was like thousands to us! Four aways she got it on. Oh God! It was like Heaven! 'Course, she spent it straight away, practically. She bought a suite for the front room, a lovely dinner service from Lambert's the posh china shop, yellows with an orange stripe, and a little pedigree dog that died.

Dad said: 'I told you so.'

He didn't believe in buying dogs. You didn't buy kiddies, did you? They came. There were plenty of dogs about Stratford looking for a good home.

'Yes,' she said, 'that's what's worrying me.' She said to me: 'You can 'ave a party! A *twenty-first!*'

I got in a flap, then!

'I ain't twenty-one, Mam!'

I wasn't, but I'd always dreamt of a twenty-first.

'You want one don't you?'

She was determined I was going to have it.

'Yes.'

So I had a party in our dining room, well, the front room. It was the first time we'd ever used it, to eat in or anything; we used the living room always. There was this very nice suite, and a sideboard our Else had got off one of her ladies, some carpet the old headmistress had left. Our Mother's new service was on display; we never used that either—no fear!

The guests arrived. They weren't *my* friends, 'cept *him*, they were Cyril's! It was more an extension of the card sharp parties: our Cyril and all his pals as used to come and play cards, Arch Sweet, Brock Brookes and Jim, they all came over from the pub. So you can imagine, they were three parts.

She'd bought a Hornby trainset for Bert, and guess what our Mother bought me? A new pianna, with bronze candle holders! That was typical—I couldn't play a note! And a cake. Now we had a nice settee in that front room, part of the suite, never sat on as a rule, but you know how they are, young chaps. They sat on it, put their feet on it, and then one of them put a cigarette down it. She came in, with the cake. It was a big un! They put it in the fender, it was so big, that cake, lowered it down, and all those candles, flickering.

'Come on Mary! Blow em out an let's 'ave a bit!'

I nearly fell in the fender trying to blow those bloody candles out. Dad was chuckling. Our Mother seemed not to mind about the settee; she was puffing away at a fag herself! I couldn't believe my eyes.

'Don't mind if I do!'

They were all laughing and joking; one of them tried to play the pianna and Dad sang a song about a Jolly Coon on his Honeymoon. Then somebody shouted: '*Fire!*'

I thought it was something to do with the candles; I was feeling a bit woozy.

> 'The porters in a mob they grab
> 'Is luggage from the 'ansom cab . . .'

I thought: What a funny smell!

It was the settee! It was on fire!

Jim came to the rescue, just in time, and Brock Brookes. They carried it into the front garden. Another minute and the house would a-burnt down—and the school!

'This is the last party I'll 'ave,' said our Mother, 'the first and the last.' But she couldn't help laughing. 'Ow d'you like it?' she said, meaning the cake. She was fond of him, she liked him coming round; that was surprising cos she wasn't one for open house, it was only our Cyril's pals got past her as a rule.

'It's lovely ta, Missus Hewins.' He grinned. Oh, he could turn on the charm unexpectedly; when you weren't expecting it you were stabbed here, in the guts.

'Hmm,' she said, 'well you stick to cake!'

She thought he drank too much; well, he did. Working at the brewery, what could you expect? It's a wonder *I* wasn't a drunk and all, cos us girls, we had to *suck* the Guinness, suck it off! We had to bottle the Guinness by hand. The chaps pinched it out the hogshead—it came from Ireland in barrels—siphoned it out with a tube, on the sly. But us girls had to sit with a sack over our legs in *front* of the blooming barrel, with six copper tubes, and suck and suck. You know how a little pig sucks its mother? We had to pull the bloody stout off like that: six copper tubes, six copper tits. When it got to the top of the bottle . . . you shut it off, *quick!* Otherwise you was swilled.

The smell wouldn't go away; you had to wash and wash. When I thought about the brewery sometimes I shivered. There's got to be something else, *something!* I wanted to ask him why *he* worked there. He needn't a-done. If you've been to grammar school you can work *any*where. I wished I could a-talked to him about it, but how can you describe feelings? We didn't talk much.

He said: 'Cheer up! Cross Keys tommorrer night?'
I said 'Yes.'
And I cried inside with wanting, even though I sensed he was growing away from me.

A funny thing, the settee was still burning inside when I went out next morning, smouldering.

Chapter Eleven

I heard two girls talking and one of them said: 'Try gin 'n' quinine.'
So I thought I would. I hadn't told our Mother, she didn't know
then. I sat upstairs; I was doing it on my own, trying. The quinine
was a white powder; you got it from the chemist's, for toothache.
Our Cyril—he was in the same room, and Bert, cos there was only
two bedrooms at the school house, our Mother and Dad was in the
other one—he said: 'What's up with our Mary, Mam?'
'I dunno.'
'What's er drinkin like that for?'
You could tell he was shocked. I thought: The times I've laid in bed
with my hands over my ears while *you* was bein sick in this po, Cyril
Hewins!
'Er's *drunk*, Mam!'
I was. I was drunk for three days, sick drunk; just my luck. I never
touched a drop since. I thought: I'll go to the doctor. I felt so ill. I'd
only been to the doctor once before. There were two brothers at the
surgery; I prayed I'd get the one who'd done my eyes, cos I knew
him. Fate was against me all the way: it was the other one!
'What's wrong with you?'
I panicked. He was so young, sort of pompous. How could I tell
him? I said: 'I've got bad headaches.'
He gave me a check-up. All the time I was thinking: Is e goin to
guess? I wished I'd never come. He looked mystified. Oh, if only it
was the other one! *E'd* a-guessed! He'd guessed 'bout my eyes.
'That all you got Miss Hewins?'
'Yes,' I said.
So he told me to go and buy some pills for my head. He was right
really, I did need my head seen to—for not speaking the truth.

I sat by the fire watching our Mother peeling apples. It was
Christmas, plum pudding time. I never seen anybody peel apples like
our Mother. The skin was off, and the core out—before you could

blink! She got the cores out, complete, with a little bone. She had a little hollow marrow bone, that's what she used for coring apples. Well, the sight of that peel curling about on the floor and on her lap . . . I had to go out.

When I came back she said: 'You'd better *tell* im.'

Our Mother was a remarkable person. That's all she said. She didn't carry on at me; she didn't fuss. She went on peeling the apples. All she said was: 'You'd better tell im.'

❖

So I did. And soon as I told him . . . I wished I hadn't! He didn't say anything. He just looked at me and went quiet. He was shocked. Then he didn't call at the house so much; it started to drop off. How did *I* feel? I'll tell you. I turned to ice inside with the dread of not seeing him and the dread of seeing him changed towards me. I'd read the signs; I knew he'd been waiting for an excuse, I knew better'n he knew himself. I couldn't keep him, that was all. It was like trying to keep a fox. Bert had, once. He'd caught a fox cub up the railway, made a pen; it was a marvel how he looked after it, loved it. But that fox scraped and scraped and scraped till it had made a hole big enough to escape. That's all it wanted to do: escape.

Our Mother said: 'What's up?'

'It's 'is mother. Er's against it.'

'Huh!'

'Er says we ain't good enough, Mam. We ain't respectable. Well, that's what er says: I'm a scruff!' I said: 'I'm *not*, Mam!' I was miraculously clean, always. That was what hurt so, when he said, 'My mother says you're a scruff.'

'You're better 'n *any* o' *them*!' Our Mother was pink with anger. 'I could tell you a thing or two 'bout er. Oighty toity cow.'

'I know,' I said, 'e told me.'

He hadn't. It was our Jim's wife, she came from Wilmcote and she'd told me his Dad was an old toff who'd got an *important* job in Brum—and another wife there and all, she reckoned. He'd hid his secret family away in that tumbledown cottage—well, it looked tumbledown to me, all trees and creepers, at the bottom of a little lane—and every day they must a-lived in dread that somebody'd find out. 'Course, they all knowed 'bout it in Wilmcote; as Jim's wife said, you can't keep secrets in a place that size, even if you can in Brum.

When *he* was eight, he was their only kiddie, they'd sent him to the Grammar School, at Stratford, *paid!*

'Oh 'is Dad was proud of im,' she said, 'you could tell. And e loved *er*. She was striking lookin, ever so *elegant*.'

'*Er!*'

'Well she was then. It was very *romantic*,' Jim's wife said. 'Then one day the old man didn't get off the train . . . She left the village, went to live in that Theatre cottage on Waterside. She lives for *im* now . . .'

My heart turned over.

'E's a *love child*, and Mother's love,' Jim's wife reckoned, 'is a terrible load.'

I asked our Mother: 'D'you think e did it just to shock *er*? I mean, go out with me?'

'If e did,' she said, 'e '*as* done it in a dish, 'asn't e?' She was quite upset; she'd liked him. 'Give im time. E's a nice lad, deep down. E'll come round.'

There she was wrong! I knew better. She wasn't always right. She never knew 'bout *him*. I didn't understand him, well, nobody did, but I knew him. I knew more about him than she did—or anybody. I knew in my heart that he wanted to escape. I just kept praying nobody would find out, 'specially our Jim.

Jim's wife said: 'I won't tell im, don't worry.' She knowed what would happen if she did. She said, 'I've got an address in Brum. But I think it's too late.'

I went to the Parish Church. I didn't go in, it weren't that sort o' church. I just walked round and round the outside, praying. I wondered about the river, 'course I did. But I was too afraid.

*

The foreman at the brewery was a man called Jack Timms. He lived on Park Road and he didn't like me. Well, I was a bit flighty, you know, I used to answer him. When I was little I'd used to call after him. He was a bloke who held grudges, stored them up; a discontented man. He liked to think he was all powerful. At the bottling end he might a-been, but down Park Road . . .

He'd say: 'You can go on washin machine today, Hewins!'

I didn't like it; I tossed my head. 'I ain't a-goin on washer!'

There was an argument then! 'I'll bloody *make* you!'

He'd put me on smelling the bottles—you can imagine—smelling the bottles when they came back from the pubs. He knew it made me heave. Or looking for mothers. *Mothers*? We used to call them that. They lurked in the bottom of bottles, looked alive, like slimy slugs. Jack Timms had it in for me.

One day me and Beat Crowe and Kate took some beer down to the messroom. Now that was a funny thing: Kate was so fat I never suspected *she* was expecting and all! Yes, Kate worked right up to having it, all that time, washing the stoppers, and nobody knew anything about it. But me! I was fated! Jack Timms had a glint in his eye. I should a-guessed when he said: 'Go down and fetch em up, will yer?'

That was the trap! He never spoke polite to you, normally. He used to tell us to fetch the older ones up cos they went down to the messroom to have a smoke—and a drink!

'Go 'n' fetch em up,' he said, 'they bin long enough down there!'

We took a bottle each, in our hands, never thought, you did it automatic.

He caught me on the stairs. 'What you doin wi that?'

'I dunno.'

He said: 'I shall 'ave to report you.'

I got the sack. I didn't get it for stealing, I got the sack cos I wouldn't let on why I was taking beer down to the messroom. All I'd say was I took it down there; I wouldn't say what it was for.

Gargy Court the manager left Jack Timms to do it. He wouldn't a-missed it for the world, anyway!

'You know you ain't s'pposed to drink on the job?'

He smiled. He *knew* I didn't! Talk about ironical! I didn't drink beer, and I got the sack for drinking! All the others drank like fishes, all the older uns; before breakfast some of them was drinking!

Kate and Beat got out of it. How? Praps they put the blame on me. Praps he cast a blind eye. They'd got a lot of relations working at the brewery; he couldn't afford to upset them all, could he? I told Beat. I laughed and said: 'You two oughta 'ad the sack 'n' all, Beat! Same as me!' It was mysterious to me how they got out of it.

But I didn't argue with Jack Timms. I thought: it's an *opening*, really. It saved giving my notice in. I'd have had to a-left, the babby would a-started to show—think how he'd a-crowed over that! And I couldn't a-got no dole, then.

*

The dole office was in Brum Road, a little shed by the canal. There was queues of folks! Men, women, old uns, young uns, all sorts. I didn't want them to take me, but I didn't want them to know *why*. They kept sending me away for jobs—the roughest ones they could find—cleaning jobs, cleaning public houses. I couldn't escape from bloody beer! But I was getting to be crafty. When I got there I'd say, 'I never done this sort o' work, mister!' or: 'I come from brewery, missus,' hinted, see. I made out I was too rough for their rotten job.

'Oh,' they said, 'well I don't think you're quite suitable.'

But then the dole office sent me to the Horse and Jockey. Out came the usual story. She was a nice woman.

'Ow old are you duck?'

I looked at the floor, all sawdust, worse'n the school: gob, beer, the lot—horrible.

'Ah, it could do wi a good go,' she said, 'nobody's bin on it since Sat'day.'

'Could I use your toilet missus?'

It was worse in there! I didn't care; I felt I was dying. The worst of it was, I couldn't get the bile out: retch, retch, retch, but nothing came up. Nerves, praps. When I got back, I told her, quick:

'I got sack from brewery!'

Well, I had to say it to get out of the job, I was desperate to get out of it.

'I won't be no good to you.'

'You sit down duck,' she said.

Oh God! I thought, I've overdone it! Er's goin to take me on out o' kindness! Er's took a fancy to me!

Sure enough, she patted my arm. But to my surprise she said: 'I'm goin to tell em you's *most* unsuitable. Now where's your paper?'

I felt myself going red. How'd she guessed? You couldn't *see*. I was about six months, but I'd been starving myself, practically, to keep thin. I used to get a sheet, rip up an old sheet, bind it round myself, tight. And I had a short coat, trimmed with fur—well, rabbit.

'You take care of yourself. And the babby.'

I could have died! She signed the paper and I thanked her and rushed out.

You see, if I'd refused a job I wouldn't a-got any dole. It wasn't much, but I did get some, I got a bit o' dole. I was still working at the school, o' course, but I didn't get paid for that.

Chapter Twelve

He still called at the school house: not very often, now and then. It was as if he couldn't stay away *al*together. He liked the family, I think—there was always a lot of comings and goings at our house— our Mother. He liked to come and sit in the larder, while she was working. What they talked about I do not know; not me, cos he made her laugh.

'E's a case, that lad,' she'd say, 'worse'n your Dad.' When I *looked*, she said: 'You didn't know im afore the war. E was different then.'

Sometimes he seemed so—*comfortable*—I started to wonder: Praps she's right! Praps he is coming round!

We'd all reckoned without Jim.

Dad told us how it happened. He was picking up the glasses in the Dragon when who should stroll in, Dad said, bold as brass, but our Mary's chap. That's what he called him: 'our Mary's chap', or 'Ginger Nut'.

'Ginger Nut
Fell in the cut . . .'

Our Mother would shake her head and laugh and go grave and say: 'Ah. E'll come a cropper. I've seen it afore. It's 'is *hair*.' She said: ' 'Is fancy words won't protect im.'

What fancy words? I wondered. He never talked to me, hardly.

Well, bold as brass into the Dragon, into the dragon's mouth he strolled, and 'course there was our Jim, looking for trouble.

Jim shouts: 'You go over the road 'n' see my sister! You go 'n' see my sister—*now*!'

It was as if we was his personal property! He was the same with everybody. He was determined to win you back for King and family; trouble was, he didn't ask you first if you *wanted* to be rescued. Years before he'd tried to frighten off our Else's Tom. They'd had a terrible fight on the railway bank, stopped all the trains, cos Tom was an engine driver and Jim was so provoking he'd had to stop his train and get out.

He was all bluster, our Jim, when he'd been boozing, but it never seemed to affect his strength. He was good looking and he was very strong. You always felt proud to have a brother like Jim.

'Go on!'

'I'll go when I'm ready.'

'You what?'

'I'll go when I'm ready.' He didn't say he'd *never* go, Dad said, he just said: 'I'll go when I'm ready.' That haunted me, after, that *'when I'm ready.'*

Jim saw red. 'Outside!' he shouted.

'Alright.'

And he went outside with our Jim.

As I said, he was well made, but our Jim was a man, and fighting mad. He loved a fight; I think it was that more'n hate, or protecting me. It was the opportunity to have a scrap. He might even a-*liked* him, really! That's Jim.

He beat him up. He beat him up outside the Dragon there, in the yard, from the yard onto the pavement, from the pavement into the middle of the main road. It stopped all the traffic.

He fought back, Dad said, but you couldn't help feeling he'd been half *expecting* it, from the start. His money went spinning wild over the road—pennies 'n' sixpences 'n' shillings. Blood spurted everywhere. His clothes was ripped. Nobody called the police; nobody cared for him, really. He wasn't one of us. They stood and watched and when our Jim had done his worst somebody picked him up and they took him to his mother's house, on Waterside.

*

The next night Jim said: 'I done it Mam! The bugger never turned up for work! E got the thrashin of 'is life!'

Just like a cat dropping a mangled body on the step for her to say 'Oh very good! What a clever pussy cat!' our Jim said: 'I done it Mam!'

Dad said: 'E did! E takes after your Harry 'n' no mistake.'

Harry Bayliss our Mother's only brother was a legend in our family. He was s'pposed to have knocked out the bloke in the booth at the Mop—in *one*! He was killed in the war through not having his helmet on.

'E was the strongest man I ever seen, Harry Bayliss,' Dad used to

64

tell us, when we were kiddies, 'but e forgot to put 'is 'elmet on. Once, that did it. Only once.'

I thought: I hope you're all bloody satisfied! I went down to Waterside, I nearly winded myself getting there. I leaned against one of the trees, watching his mother's house, hoping, praying, you know, for a sign of life.

People went by to the Theatre. I waited till it was quite dark. The Theatre had started ages ago. Someone had told me she worked at the Box Office. It wasn't true, but I didn't know. I thought: She's bound to come out! I don't know what I was planning to do, or say. I didn't care! I'd lost all my fear of her. I thought: She's bound to come out soon! But she didn't. The Theatre looked dead, how it does when a play's on. There was no smoke from the house—nothing. It was all as dead as a doornail.

He'd gone. I knew he'd gone. Oh how pleased she'd be, how she would enjoy saying: 'I told you—scruffs!' I walked up and down Waterside and I thought my heart would break.

A week after, Jim said: 'The bugger's sent for 'is cards, from away! I done it Mam! E's *gone!*'

*

Both our rooms at the school house, the living-room and the front room, had painted tiles round the fireplace. I used to sit and say to myself, oh for hours: 'Spring, Summer, Autumn, Winter . . .' There were four lovely ladies, with bonnets on. When it was Spring there were flowers; when it was Winter there she was, still only in a dress but huddled up a little. Spring, Summer, Autumn, Winter, Spring, Summer—Oh God! *June.* That's when it was due.

Then it came to me in a flash, and I wondered why I hadn't thought of it before. I said aloud: 'That ud be the answer, Mam!'

'Wot?'

'Adoption.'

'Answer for oo?'

I could see she didn't approve, but she said: 'You must please yourself.'

There was a girl I knew who'd had one adopted. She gave me an address, and I wrote. I was determined. They sent me papers and things—complicated!—I couldn't understand the *words!* But I kept thinking: It'll ruin my life, else. There was no-one to ask. Vicar? We kept away from him, never used to let him come near, let him see us.

65

Doctor? I'd told him a lie. I didn't know *any*body educated. I was on my own.

Well, nearly. There was a knock on the door. I saw a shape; through the panes I saw a big black shape—tall! It was a chap! My heart missed a beat. I went without thinking—that's the story of my life—and there stood a tramp.

'Could I 'ave some water please, ma'am?'

He was a real old tramp, from the workhouse, with cans, billy cans, and a sack. They were a common sight still in Stratford. I told him to wait there, fetched the kettle.

'I'm sorry,' he said, 'was you expectin somebody else?'

He wore the filthiest old coat you ever seen; his hat looked as if it had been rolled in cowshit. But his ribbons! He had a row of ribbons, all colours of the rainbow, and his voice was, you know, like running water.

'It's a marvellous and terrible world,' he said, 'to be bringin a little child into. Beg your pardon, you ain't got nothin stronger 'ave you?'

'It won't 'ave a Dad.'

I don't know what made me tell *him*!

His face changed. 'That could be an advantage ma'am,' he said. 'Didn't do some well-known folks much 'arm. Think about it.'

'I 'ave done.'

After that he called fairly regular. He had a round, most of them did: Warwick, Stratford, Alcester. Once he turned up with an old woman. It was the old workhouse round; they'd got into the habit, I 'spect, couldn't stop. He was quite harmless, took an interest in me, God knows why. I only gave him water, never let him further'n the porch.

He talked in poetry. 'I learned em by heart,' he said, 'so I don't need no book. Keep em 'ere!' he said. 'It's summat they can't tek off you.'

Then one day he didn't come; I never saw him again.

Chapter Thirteen

It was a Friday night. I had to move the desks every Friday night, when the kiddies had gone. They were big iron desks, well, iron feet with solid wood tops, terrible double desks: two sat in them. I had to drag them to the front of the classroom, put wet sawdust down and sweep the floor. Dad helped, did what he could. It was boards, that floor, dreadful, sometimes a kiddie had been sick, and all the time I was thinking: There's the polishin, an those bloody glass partitions to clean an dust, an the winder sills.

I was tired as hell. I remember Dad saying: 'Yer Mam's worse. She should 'ave the operation,' but all I could think was: There's more'n fifty of them towels to wash, an the dusters, an you'll be buggerin off any minute now! He'd do his share, Dad, I'll say that, help with the desks when I asked. But then he'd be edging off, towards the Dragon.

'She likes it 'ere.'

I thought: What's all this in aid of?

'She loves it in the school house, she's happy 'ere. Well,' he said, 'I'll be off then, duty calls. I'm promised tonight.'

It was true! Our Mother did love it! She loved to see the people going by to the station, all the comings and goings. I was glad somebody did! I gave one of those desks a shove . . . and that was it!

'Oh my God!' I said. It was the surprise more'n anything—water gushing. I shouted aloud. I was on my own; nobody could hear me. Our Mother was in the school house and Cyril sleeping. He was on shifts, at the flour mill. Water was gushing down my legs onto the floor, and I knew then what it was, I sensed it. I kept saying: 'Oh my God.' I got out of the school somehow. It was a terrible feeling, not being in charge of your body. There was something else—some*body* else—trying to get out! Horrible!

Our Mother must a-*known*: she was coming down the stairs. When she seen me holding myself she said: 'You better lie down.' Then she shouted for our Cyril, she knocked him up! 'Fetch Ede. Tell er water's broke,' she said, '*quick*!' Her calling to Cyril like that really put the wind up me. If she was getting him out o' bed, our Cyril, it was serious!

And that's how he was born: in the school house, after I'd been moving the desks, before I'd filled in those blooming adoption papers. You could say he beat me to it. The pains weren't bad, well, he was so small. The doctor was saying—Cyril'd had to fetch doctor 'n' all in the end, I had to have stitches—he was saying: 'She ain't bin eatin! Why ain't she bin eatin?' And: 'It'll be touch'n' go. She's a very foolish girl, she's bin holdin erself in.'

It was the same doctor! I thought: Does e remember? What'll e *think*?

'Look!' said Ede. She lifted the babby up and showed him me, all blood and yolk. 'E's got no finger nails, the little duck! E's come out the egg too soon!' He had! Six weeks too soon! 'But 'is 'air's lovely! Fancy! Look at 'is 'air!'

Mother and Dad looked at each other. I knew what they were thinking. Nobody in our family had hair like that.

I wanted to die.

Monday morning as usual the Vicar came. He came to the school, there was always hymns and prayers, then he sent for Dad who said: 'Good news! There's a babby been born!'

'So I 'ear,' said the Vicar, 'and I wants it *out*, this day, this minute, Hewins! *And* er! Else your job goes, and the house!'

Dad dropped his shovel. He *had* to, he said, or it would a-come down over the Vicar's head. And he went to break the news to our Mother. I heard them talking, in the larder.

Our Mother starts shouting: 'She ain't a-goin!'

'Don't worry, our Mary,' said Ede, 'I'll 'ave you.'

Well, I was a-sobbing, I was frit, you can imagine. Jess had died; why couldn't I?

Ede had her ear pressed to the door. 'Dad's gone for Doctor!'

I didn't see how that was going to help. I was thinking: 'She's got a houseful already! She took in everybody in our family who hadn't got a roof. There was always somebody at our Ede's, not just one at a time neither, and she had plenty of her own. It was only a tiny council house. God, I thought, I don't want to go up there. But Dad managed it, somehow; he fetched the doctor back. There weren't half a Kerfuffle.

The doctor was excited and all. His voice was raised: 'The room's clean. She's got help. Where's the objection?'

Our Mother told him.

He said: 'I'll see 'bout this! That girl's not to be moved! It'll kill em both. *Christians!*' he said.

I never heard no more about it. I don't know whether Doctor Pembrey saw the Vicar, but I think he must a-done. I never heard a word about us having to go, after.

*

That's why we went to Shottery to have him christened. The Vicar wouldn't do it—well, we didn't ask him. We knew he'd say 'no'.

Dad said, 'We won't give im the *satisfaction*.'

So we went to Shottery, after work. I stopped by the stile; I wouldn't go farther, to the church, I was too ashamed.

'I'll wait 'ere,' I said.

Tom Dyke carried him and the others followed; he was too quick for them, whistling away. Our Ede's Tom was a happy chap. He hadn't got a bean but he was the happiest chap I knowed.

I thought: That could be a good sign.

Tom first, then Else who was going to be godmother, and Dad.

'What's '*is* Dad doin?' I wondered. What's e doin now? But I kept my thoughts to myself.

Coming back over the fields they were in the same order, only Else had the babby.

'Ooo!' she said, 'ain't it 'ot?' and: 'E ain't 'alf 'eavy! 'Ere, you can 'ave im now.'

It was hot that evening, hot August. Else held a buttercup under his chin:

'E's goin to be rich!' she said.

They all laughed. That buttercup had took some finding! Even I had to laugh. But I couldn't help thinking 'bout *him*—and Sis. What does she think of me? I wondered. I dreaded her mouth. I dreaded what she'd say. She was married, she'd had a fella alright, seen a man in all his glory. It seemed a long time since *I* had. Yes, I'll confess it, I was aching in my heart for him, I would a-done anything to see him, hear his voice, feel him, anything. I knowed it was wrong, wicked, but you can't help *feelings*.

I was in a daze; there were so many feelings spinning round in my head. Oh and it was hot! We seemed to be walking on the sky, and the grass and the trees growing downwards. There was a spell on everything that summer's night.

When we got home our Jim was there and he said to our Mother:

69

'I'm goin to kill im. Next time I catches im I'll kill im.'

'Where's e buggered off to?' she said. But she meant Dad. 'I've made the tea! They ain't gone to Dragon—'ave they?'

He had! And Tom! By the look on our Else's face she'd a-been there and all—if she'd dared!

As I said, Else stood godmother, Tom Dyke was his godfather. We called him Brian. I don't know why, it just came to me. I broke the royal tradition. At the registry I'd asked for *Bryan*, but the woman there looked down her nose and said:

'That's not ow you spell it. It's B-R-I-A-N.'

Being an early child he looked, you know, *old*, but his hair! He had red gold hair, it caught in the sun. Nobody ever said, aloud, but he was the spit image.

Ede and Else was whispering: 'S'weird, innit?'

'No mistakin.'

'Poor little duck.'

I was frit to death nobody would love him, except me.

I hadn't wanted to. For days after he was born I hadn't even wanted to look at him. I wouldn't touch him. The resemblance! I couldn't bear it.

Our Mother said: 'E's sickin up tinned stuff. E's gettin no nourishment. If e don't get proper nourishment soon, e'll *die*.'

'Let im!' I thought.

They never weighed him when he was born. She wouldn't let them, said he was too tiny, it was tempting fate, bad luck. There was quite a battle with a nurse who came.

'You gotta 'ave im weighed, missus! E's *premature*.'

'E's our babby, not your'n. It's a free country ain't it?' But she kept hounding *me*! 'You'll 'ave to feed im!'

'I can't Mam, I can't!'

The *idea* made me heave!

She said: 'You'll 'ave to. You'll 'ave to try.'

So I did. I didn't want to, I didn't want to love him. But as soon as he was there, at my breast, soon as I'd felt his little hands and his little mouth, I thought: E's mine! E's all mine!

It was the most wonderful feeling I'd ever had. I used to sit out in the yard there, in the sun, nursing him for hours and hours. It was the school holiday, the kiddies had gone. There was only the sound of the hens chuck-chucking. Oh it was the last long hot peaceful summer.

Chapter Fourteen

There was a family conference in our larder. Well, it was more our Mother making up her mind and telling us. She used to do her baking in the larder. It was like a small room, with big wide whitewood shelves and a whitewood table where she could work. That was all she did now, really, the baking—she was in so much pain—I did the rest of the housework and the school. The others came and helped when they could.

We all squashed in. Her hands! She had big hands but she was light as a feather with pastry. Oh her pies! Her puddings! She was a miraculous cook, our Mother, she could make a pudding out of nothing! She never weighed *anything*; there were no scales in our house. And something else! She could skin a rabbit in one piece, with the head on, so's we got full price at Warburton's! Break the legs, roll the skin back: it came off perfect, like a glove.

Our Mother was in command in that larder. She never let me *touch*. The result was, I never did know how to bake proper, I was never handy 'bout the house, only the cleaning, the rough stuff. She never let me *near*! Only to finish the bowl off with my finger, or lick the custard pan. Now I was grown, with a kiddie of my own, but it was just the same.

' 'Ere y'are!'

That's how she saw us all: as kiddies.

Everybody was there, 'cept George, and Flo of course, she was in London. I thought: Oh God! Our Flo's comin down to Stratford for safety! That's what it was about: the *war*. Our Mother said there'd be one; she could read the signs. Well, we'd had a letter come round asking if we'd got any spare sheets. Spare sheets! That was a laugh. We made nappies out of the old uns.

I dreaded it: the thought of asking for strap, and Flo taking our bed, and Flo's two lads with appetites like billy goats champ-champ-champ through everything: 'Mam's told us to eat as much as we can!'

Our Mother said: 'You'll 'ave to 'ave im up.'
They were all looking at *me*!
'No!'
'It's the only way—'
'Kate never!'
Kate had hers 'bout the same time as Brian, at her sister's. It had been a surprise to everybody, her sister and all.
Ede said: 'If you don't they'll say you been with Mop men—'
'Bein a Whit un.'
'You gotta do it.'
'No!' I said. I couldn't bear the thought of going to court.
Our Mother said: 'If you don't, there's no knowing what folks'll say.'
'You gotta go out *some*time!'
'For '*is* sake!'
'*Mam's*!'
' 'Elp with the money!'
I wouldn't go out. After he was born I never went out the school for months; well, I was too ashamed. I thought people would be talking about me.
'I *can't*!'
'You should 'ave *some*thing,' our Mother said, 'then folks'll know you ain't a tramp. If you take im to court it'll show you ain't a tramp. That's settled then.'
I thought: They'll never find him.
It was my only hope.

*

He wouldn't look.
The solicitor did. He took one look at Brian, said quick: 'Bring the child to court, *in case*.' He meant in case he denied it. So Dad waited outside with him, in the passage at the Town Hall. He was good as gold. But he didn't want to see him, he didn't want to see his own child, he wouldn't look at him.
Right! I thought, I won't look at *you*!
I just looked at this woman on the bench, this Justice of the Peace. I kept my eyes fixed on her and I gave evidence. I kept telling myself: It shows I know oo 'is father is. If I'd just a-let it go . . . The funny thing was, I wasn't frit, I was blazing! The newspapers was there, writing it all down, what I said, the private private things, so's people could crow over it and say, 'Shockin!' or 'She was headin for a fall!'

I'd always been so smartly dressed, you see, it annoyed them. Let them! I thought, let them say! I wouldn't look at him; I was blazing with anger.

He didn't deny it. He just said: 'I'm very young, Sir.'

It was seven-and-six.

He never paid, half the time.

I had to go to the town clerk's office, in Sheep Street.

' 'As e paid?'

'No!' they said, with a smirk on their faces, those girls at Lunn's. I had to go there for it; he sent the money to Tom Lowth, at Lunn's. I went every month. Tom Lowth was a gentleman, but they were snooty girls; they looked down their noses at you. I had to say: 'Mary Hewins. 'Ave I got any money?'

They could hardly be bothered to look in the book.

'No!'

They didn't want to know, they looked through you like, and then they'd shove you out. That broke me down where the Magistrates and the papers hadn't. Once I came home in tears, I was feeling so depressed, and Dad said: 'I'll go.'

After that he went a lot for it, with the pram—he never minded what people said—and fetched my money. He always seemed to be more successful than me.

When we did get some—oh that was a field day! We could buy something: food, mostly. Seven-and-six a week! There was never more'n two pound something waiting at Lunn's, but it was better'n nothing! It did show he'd got a father, didn't it? My milk had dried up. That was no great surprise, well I was so thin! So he had to have cow's milk, from a little dairy on Greenhill Street. A Mrs Davies kept it; she had a green apron and a nice rosy face. One day our Ede rushes round:

'Ey, that little girl at "Thatch"—er's sick! Mortal! They say Mother Davies's sellin *consumptive milk*!'

It worried me to death. She'd been born the same week as Brian, that little girl. Her Mam and Dad ran the Thatched Tavern. Well, she died, and you can see her statue in the cemetery: an angel. When I go by I always think of those days. I dreaded TB. Her name was Beck; she was eight months old. But Brian lived.

*

He hadn't paid for a long time, so we had to have him up again. He said he'd broke his leg; he came with his leg bound up, dragging it. He always was a bit of an actor. I looked the other way. If I look, I thought, if I catch his eye, I might weaken.

He said: 'I can't work!'

Even his voice, quiet and deep . . . I had to sit down, have some water.

The Magistrate said to him: ' 'Ave you eaten today?'

'Yes.'

'Well your babby's gotta eat 'n' all.'

It didn't make any difference.

He'd left Stratford, for good. Some said he'd gone Stroud way, over the Cotswolds: his mother had relations there. Some said he'd been called up. He'd took to the road, joined a theatre company. Praps it was true; praps he did break his leg.

I wonder.

*

When the air raid siren sounded I ran upstairs for Brian, grabbed him. I said: 'We'll 'ave to get to shelter Mam!' It was up by the workhouse, they'd got air raid shelters up there. I forgot about the gasmasks. I wasn't half in a panic. Our Mother said: 'You're better off 'ere. You stay 'ere,' and: 'You ain't takin *im*.'

'I thought it meant you'd gotta run 'n' get in the shelter?'

'Never mind what it *means*,' said our Mother, 'you stay 'ere. It'll be alright.'

I believed her! Well, you didn't argue with our Mother. I stayed, but I was in such a panic. I panicked when that siren sounded; I panicked when it stopped. I panicked when the 'All Clear' went. '*All Clear!*' Your stomach went with it, like the chairoplanes at the Mop. But she was right: it never sounded again.

That was all we had of the war, till one night when I got home our Mother said: 'I'm just goin out for some chips.'

She didn't do much cooking now. The pain had got so bad she couldn't bother, even for Cyril. Our Cyril's hot supper was coming from the chip shop. That was a bad sign.

She got to the front door—and she was thrown back!

'God,' she said, 'that shook me!'

There was a noise like old sheets being ripped up. Coventry was on.

Next morning they started coming into the hospital or just walking to Stratford, for safety.

'It's *gone*,' Dad said, 'the whole bloomin city, blasted off the face of the earth! A chap told me.' He was very upset. He said, 'I'll go to buggery!'

I held on to Brian, tighter and tighter.

'Ey praps they won't bomb 'ere cos of *Shakespeare*!'

'There's Alum.'

'That munitions place our Else works at!'

'S'only a shed!'

'Jerry wouldn't waste 'is shells.'

I thought, sudden: They shouldn't a-put im down the well! It's a punishment.

Dad said what I was thinking: 'Why should e bother 'bout Shakespeare?'

When we didn't? You see, some of the young chaps had found a big crate on the sidings, ever so heavy. When they got it opened—lo and behold—it was *Shakespeare*! Hundreds of complete Shakespeares.

Dad laughed when he heard about it. He said: ' "Good Attendance" prizes!'

What he meant by that I do not know.

They were so disappointed. They put him down the brewery well, and there he is, to this day.

Bert said: 'I've put in for Navy! I've been to the recruitin office only they wants to see me birth certificate, Mam.'

'Huh.'

'I'm old enough! They said I can be a boy sailor!'

A funny look came over our Mother's face. She said: 'Alright then, please yourself.'

'Wot?' Dad hit the roof, nearly.

'You 'eard im. E's old enough.'

'E'll be *exempt* where e is! You said it yourself. "Our Bert'll be exempt!" '

'Well,' she said, 'I've changed my mind. If e wants to be a boy sailor e can bloody well be one.'

Next morning she gave him his birth certificate, in an envelope. Bert rushed off. It was always his great ambition, to go to sea; nobody ever knew why. You couldn't be much further from it 'n Stratford. Dad reckoned it was on account of a trip he'd took him on once, to Weston.

'You never seen a kiddie so en*joy* himself as our Bert, that day at Weston!'

I knew what he meant. Bert's happy days stuck in your mind. Half an hour later he was back. 'I hate you!' he cried, and he burst into tears. Bert idolized our Mother, so it was a shock when he said: 'I *hate* you! I'll hate you for ever!'

She flushed, bit her lip.

I didn't find out for weeks, when Bert had got over it; he did, of course. But for weeks he wouldn't speak to her. It seems she'd writ a letter, put it in with the certificate.

'Why did she do it?' Bert said. '*Why*?'

He was under age, the letter said, she was his guardian, and she would never give her permission for him to go to be a boy sailor, and if they took him . . . just let them try . . .

'Oh,' said Bert, 'the shame! I'll never be able to hold my head up in the street again! *Every*body'll know!'

'Don't be so daft,' I said, though I was a fine one to talk.

Chapter Fifteen

They'd all took to Brian. To think I'd worried whether anybody would!

'Can I take Brian out?'

'I'll 'ave our Brian today, Mam!'

You know how some kiddies are? Always laughing, sort of blessed? As if they've been kissed by a good fairy? That was Brian when he was a babby. It was a marvel how they'd *all* took to him, and they'd got kiddies of their own, even Marg, and she wasn't really family. That caused a bit of jealousy.

Else said: 'I wouldn't leave im up there, our Mary!'

'She's only bein kind!'

She was; Marg was very kind. She was a bit, you know, airy fairy, but she came regular to do our washing. Dad did the nappies—I could never face doing that, or changing him—and Marg did the rest.

Else said: 'I'll take Gwendoline'—that was her little girl, she was seven—'and 'ave a walk up the Swincotes, just to make *sure*.'

She came back with the pram. 'I told you!' She said: 'I picked im up and e was soakin wet! So I changed im and e put 'is arms round me neck'—she loved him, our Else—'and I said: "Marg, I'm takin our Brian back 'ome."'

Dad lifted him out so's he could put the coal in. He lifted him so gently, like a chick, like this! When we moved to the school house the Vicar said: 'Use the church coal, Hewins, at your discretion.' We *did*! Our Ede went home with a pramful, always, so did Else. Today she looked a bit flushed. I thought: I do 'ope she 'asn't offended Marg! I liked Marg, even if she was in a world of her own.

Else said: 'I've just seen 'is other grandmother!'

We were all ears.

'She tried to look in the pram!'

'Go on!'

'Huh,' said our Mother, 'I 'ope you put the hood up.'

'I did,' said Else, 'and the apron! La-de-da bitch! Lookin as if she owned Stratford! Er face didn't 'alf change when she seen us comin! I said to im: "Your other grandmother ain't goin to see you—ever!" ' Else said: 'She might *look* like a lady . . .'

Suddenly I got frit, you know, as if a *witch* was after him. I wouldn't let go of him, all evening, and when we went to bed I laid awake for ages feeling his little heart beat on mine, like a butterfly, fluttering, so tiny, so delicate, you couldn't imagine it would survive. 'Course, then it happened: I forgot his bloody milk.

You see, when he woke and started whimpering I'd creep over to the gas ring and warm some milk. It took ages to do. 'Shh!' I'd be whispering, 'shh!' rocking him and whispering 'shh!' cos the big thing was not to wake our Cyril. Little bubbles were gathering round the side of the pan, he was whimpering and I was dead tired and . . .

I was woke by the milk going 'Whoosh!' spitting and spluttering all over the ring and Brian screaming and Cyril cussing in the room next door and our Mother muttering in her sleep: 'Not again! Can't you ever stay awake while that bloody milk boils? Cyril's on roads . . . e's gotta get up 'alf-past . . .' When Brian was born she and Dad came in with me and Bert, and Cyril went in their room, so's Cyril wouldn't be disturbed. Cyril this and Cyril that! Sometimes I thought the house was run round our Cyril's every desire. I was past crying. You know the smell of burnt milk? I thought: I'll get it off in the mornin. I crept downstairs and fetched some more.

Hours later I crawled back in. It was dreadful, really, the sleeping, cos we had to have the dog in with us as well. Now Dad could never resist a stray dog. The trouble was, *he'd* took to Brian and all! He was an old Labrador; well, Labrador cross, a lovely dog. Only thing was he hadn't got a tail. We called him Blackie. He always came and slept with me and Brian, got in first, with his head on the pillow. I had to climb over him. It was a single bed, pushed against the wall, by the lattice. Oh God!

You can imagine, I was always bleary eyed in the morning. 'Mam, I 'ad a funny dream last night.'

'So did I,' she said. Then I remembered: I'd woke her up! 'I dreamt our Cyril was disturbed. You gotta *think* of Cyril,' she said, 'e's only one earnin!' She didn't count Dad.

'Mam, I dreamt 'is other grandmother snatched the pram and we was all chasin, and things kept falling out, like bottles and sacks o' coal and a great big cheese!'

'A *what*?'

'A great big cheese, like in the Maypole. A whole un. *Round*. We all started chasin that instead of er and when we came back er'd gone. It was empty, the whole of Rother Market was empty. You never seen nothing like it. All the streets of Stratford was empty and I ran up and down, up and down, and I couldn't find a living soul—'

Our Mother said sudden: 'It's Sat'day.'

'Oh no!' Nothing was going right for me!

> Friday's dream
> Sat'day told
> Will come true
> Though ever so old

She'd always told us that, our Mother—and I'd gone and done it! She said, sharpish: 'Hanging about the house ain't doin you any good.'

I could have told her that!

'You'll 'ave to get work. We could do with the money. Asides,' she said, 'now this bloody war's on . . . you got a babby but you ain't *married*. They'll call you up—and Cyril.'

'Oh Mam!'

I didn't want to leave Brian.

'Why did that bloody flour mill 'ave to go 'n' burn down? E was safe, there.' She said, 'They'll 'ave im now e's labourin.'

'You'll think of something Mam!'

She shook her head: 'No.'

That '*no*'! My stomach—you know how it is when you realize, finally, definitely, that your Mam can't protect you, really protect you? *No*body can. Ever?

We were on our own, all of us, even our Cyril, the apple of her eye.

They put him in the Royal Artillery. All I can remember is how he hated his hat. At the station he was still pulling it about. He looked so disgusted.

'Oh you don't 'alf look *handsome*, Cyril!'

'Stop laughin!'

He couldn't do anything with it. 'It's like a bloody paper boat,' he said. 'Fancy goin to war lookin like this!'

He took Brian up and said he'd send him Hitler's balls for breakfast, something like that, and promised our Bert he'd get him a lot of German medals. Not English ones, German medals. That's what Bert wanted, till he could get some himself. He still hankered after the Navy. Cyril was avoiding our Mother's face. We all were. She must have had some thoughts, seeing him in that khaki uniform. And Dad.

'I'll be alright Mam.'

Knowing our Cyril, I could believe that. He'd never 'got on', well, what people call 'gettin on', but he was quiet and crafty. He was a quiet one, not like our Jim, who always let you know he was coming miles away—he'd been turned down, 'unfit for fighting'. What a laugh.

I said: 'Poor ole Hitler!'

Our Mother spread out her arms; she couldn't see for the tears, none of us could.

'Ow'll you manage wi the food, son?'

Chapter Sixteen

I didn't wait for a letter; I volunteered for war work. I was no heroine. I was just terrified they'd send me away if I didn't, make *me* join the army. And like our Mother said, we needed the money. So I volunteered.

They said: 'She can go to the Alum.'

I was back where I started! Square One. Only this time round it weren't pans 'n' kettles: it was aircraft bits, soldering them with a flame. Well, I think it was aircraft bits: you couldn't tell *what* you were making! That made it worse. I hated it; the heat made me ill. And I was still losing weight. Praps they were worried I'd die on them; any road, they said, quick: 'The Canning's just as good.'

I was transferred to the Canning Factory, next door.

What part did I go to? Oh God! I was put on the tables! It was piece work—that was a joke for a start, *peace* work!—so you had to work blooming hard, filling the cans: rhubarb, spinach, carrots, peas, strawberries, plums, whatever was in season. I did that at first. The fruit and veg, the raw stuff, was tipped onto a long table; then you had to scoop it up in your hands and put it in the can and put that on the line. The line took the can to the machines.

The stuff was never washed, though the spinach always seemed to be wet, but sometimes we had to top and tail it on these long tables, or chop it. Oh, chopping made your hands dreadful. I used to think: What's the worst thing—and what's the *best* thing 'bout this—or that? There's generally *some*thing. The best thing about the Canning was the smells: the fruit cooking, and the jam. And when the strawberries was in: oh that was lovely, when the strawberries came in! Mmm. We ate them, pounds 'n' pounds of them!

The worst thing was 'take off'. When the full cans left the machines two girls had to take them off, you know, lift them off and place them round great big containers. And oh it was such back-breaking work, that was! I think that was the worst. The cans were put in these great big containers; they'd got to go and be cooked, see. That was heavy work. I used to get out of it when I could. Well, I was 'in' with Ethel. She looked after the labels. She was very glamorous, Ethel, she went out with the foreman's son, so she got all the best jobs, she never soiled her hands. There was a little office for the labels . . . piles of labels, had to be checked: 'RED PLUMS' and 'YELLOW PLUMS' and 'TATERS'. They handed them out to the labeller; that's all they did in there. Ethel was very good to me. When she had to take sample cans—she did that for the travellers—she asked for me:

'I'll 'ave Mary to 'elp me.'

I got out of 'take off' as much as I could. So imagine my surprise when I got 'promoted'! I went up to the top end at the Canning! Well, I was always early. That impressed them, I s'ppose; they thought I was keen. I used to creep out early so's Brian didn't realize I'd gone. At first he used to get so upset if he found I'd gone. If he'd cried *before* I went I couldn't a-gone, I couldn't a-left him, crying. Sometimes I got there an hour early. That impressed them.

There were two girls on a machine. All the cans came along, see, you had to fill a funnel with lids. There was a girl by me stamping them, stamping what was going to be in the cans, you know, 'PLUMS A.1.', and I ran the machine. Well, one day the mechanic came by, his name was Bob, and he saw how my machine was oiled. I kept it perfect, always running, never went hot; the oil was always topped up.

He said: 'I could do with a mate.'

The other girls laughed. *Did* they! But he meant it, he asked for me. And the foreman said: 'Alright, she can go.'

That's how I came to do mechanical work. I loved it! It was something I really liked doing! I had the knack, Bob said so—and it was true. At the brewery, at the school, I'd always felt like a servant, a slave. You just thought: Another bloomin day! or: Roll on 'alf-past four! or: 'Alf-past six! I was always counting the time. I never did that when I started on mechanical work.

Bob was mechanic for the whole factory, a shy chap, quiet; he used to do all the repairs, if a machine stopped. The cans had to be kept going; they had to go round and round and round, you see, in the cooker. He'd come over from Canada, volunteered for the British army when the war started. But he weren't fit or something, too old, so they sent him to Stratford, and that's how he came to be in the Canning up the Brum Road.

I'd never felt good at anything before. Bob would say: 'What do

Lunch-break at the 'Canning' during the Second World War (Mary standing, second from right). Two girls are eating one of the factory's raw materials—carrots

you think, Mary?' He took me with him to Evesham to look for a nailing machine. They needed one for the cans; they had to be nailed into crates for the troops. We went to Evesham on the bus, had a walk about, a good laugh—lunch paid! Oh we had a lovely day! We chose it—bought it! I did some nailing then: the machine came down and nailed it, all the top, nailed the crate, nailed it beautifully.

Don't get the idea it was all work, no play! I couldn't stay serious all the time, it wasn't in my nature. That's where I was a disappointment to Bob, I think. Every morning after I'd oiled—I told you I got there early, I'd done by eight o'clock, practically—I took my oil can and my rag and went and chatted with the other girls, 'ave-you-'eard-this, 'ave-you-'eard that?

' " '*Ome Guard*" Thomas?'

Everybody laughed. It was Mrs Whickey* the manager's wife. Poor woman, we loved taking her off.

' " '*Ome Guard?*" You're never '*ere*!'

He wasn't.

I was oiling a machine and Whickey's latest girlfriend was on the other side. He hurried down the slope, he couldn't stay away for long.

I said: 'When's it *my* turn, Mister Whickey?'

I was wicked! Fortunately, he was very good-natured. He was alright to me, Whickey; he'd give me cans that was opened to take home for Brian, damaged cans and that.

Well, this morning he comes right up to me, makes a beeline for me, and I thought: You've gone too far this time Mary Hewins! I could never resist being cheeky.

He looks over his glasses at me and he whispers: 'Do you think *Gladys* 'as got over er 'usband?'

'I'll 'ave to investigate, Mister Whickey. S'only six months since e was killed. I'll let you know.'

I thought: Winnie'll be back on 'take off' next week!

Poor Whickey! We all took advantage. And when he did put his foot down he always made a cock-up of it. Like when he sent Rose Grinnell home—for talking! Rose was deaf and dumb, and she got sent home for talking, if ever you could believe it. Well, Rose always wanted to *try* to talk to you, and this day the girl on the table with her felt so sorry she had to stop and listen, or pretend to listen—so nobody was getting any work done. All the machines stopped. So Whickey sent Rose home for the day.

I laughed. I said to Whickey: 'Fancy sendin a dumb girl 'ome for *talkin*!'

He was like a kiddie in a sweetshop with all those girls and no competition much, cos the young lads got called up, fast, soon as they reached eighteen. It was his sight got him off, I 'spect: he was blind as a bat without his glasses. I know, cos one day he bent over the sugar vat to look at something—and his glasses fell in. It was the syrup for the plums. His glasses fell in and they shrivelled up before my eyes. They were never rescued.

He wasn't half in a panic. He said: 'You'll 'ave to go 'n' get us some more!'

* Pseudonym.

I said: 'Ow about the prescription?'

'Just say "Specs for Mister Whickey." ' He said: ' 'Urry up! I can't see!'

'Ullo!' said the girls when I went along with my oil can and my rag. 'We seen im give you them plums! What you shown im for that?'

'It ain't what I *showed* im . . .'

Then I told them the latest news. When I got to Gladys she'd describe everything that had gone on—'Oo-er!'—every little thing Whickey had done, the night before, and I'd pass *that* on.

'Oo-*er*!'

It was better'n *News of the World*.

And don't think the chaps didn't join in: they were the worst of the lot!

Old Tommy who stoked the boiler said: 'Er's gotta 'nother *parcel*!'

One of the girls, she was very attractive and a bit stuck up, she used to take these mysterious parcels to the incinerator. Nobody knew what was in them.

We *all* had a guess, 'course we did!

As I said, I think Bob was a bit disappointed with me; he couldn't change my nature. But I did love it, working with him. My title was 'mechanic's mate'. '*Bob's mate*,' the girls said. There was no jealousy; we was all together. I got fitted out with a blue boiler suit, and one of the girls, her young brother, he could *draw*, he pencilled a picture of me, in my boiler suit, with my oil can. Well, it weren't a proper picture, it didn't look like me much, he did it for a bit o' fun. He put it on the wall, above the machines.

The cans for the potatoes had to be lacquered. That's how it came about that Bob and me invented a lacquering machine—we made that machine, on our own! I had a pound for my help; Bob gave me a pound and he had five pound. We found the materials on the scrap heap, outside. Bob designed it; he was clever, that chap, made little pieces o' metal. I helped, drilled two holes in each of them. When we tried it, it *worked*! A big wheel went round and the lacquer was in the bottom. It was marvellous!

'This is only the start!' said Bob, 'you'll see! Next time we'll invent summat bigger 'n' better!'

We'd got all sorts of ideas.

*

At nights, when we finished, Ethel and me walked home together.

85

She lived up the Alcester Road. Dad used to bring Brian to meet us; they never got very far, only 'bout as far as the hospital gates.

'Your Brian's the spit image,' said Ethel. I knew what she was getting at, well she was curious, but I wouldn't be drawn. She was my friend, Ethel was, she was alright to me, but I thought: That's my own, I'm not sharin it. It was the only thing I never did share with anybody. Even our Mother. It was a secret room, a room only I'd got the key for. And inside . . . my secrets, laid out there. I looked at Brian on his little three wheeler and I thought: E thinks of the ole man as 'is Dad! They were inseparable. That did used to upset me, but there was nothing I could do about it.

'There goes Lieutenant Whickey!' cried Ethel, 'on manoeuvres!'

We laughed. We knew where he was off to: he'd got his Home Guard outfit on! Biking down Arden Street, he didn't half look comical, what with his specs and his helmet and all his paraphernalia.

I nearly said to her: 'I could 'ave got some sugar out this mornin, when I went to cash 'is cheque!' But I didn't.

Whickey used to send me up the town to cash his cheques; I could get out of the Canning then without being searched. They picked on so many, see, every night, to search, but Whickey sent me in the daytime.

'I'm just goin to cash Mister Whickey's cheque,' I told the man on the gate, 'and I gotta parcel to post for im.'

I looked at it and I thought: I wonder?

'What's your Brian got in 'is 'and?' said Ethel, when we got close. 'Ullo Mister Hewins!'

She got on alright with Dad. I s'ppose if you didn't have to *live* with him . . .

'We went to see the animals at Cattle Market and I've bought im a whip,' said Dad, 'it's a good un.'

Not another bloomin whip! I thought.

'Should you like a demonstration, Ethel?'

It cracked! Ethel shrieked.

'It cost seven-and-six,' said Brian.

It was my turn to shriek.

'You're only earnin two pound! You want your brains examinin, you do!'

'E fancied it,' he said. That's all he'd say: he fancied it! It was like water off a duck's back with him. 'And so do I,' he said, and winked.

Chapter Seventeen

' 'Ere they come,' said Dad.

The evacuees came to the school to be sorted out. Ever since war was declared they'd been coming, not so many now, but every time still when I seen them my heart missed a beat: little flocks of them, from Brum mostly, trooping from the station. Clothes! Shoes! Chocolate! Little grey jerseys, brand new! When I seen them I thought: I hope there's some Cadbury's *Milk*! There was a lot of Bournville always, with a red label, but Brian didn't like the plain, he liked milk.

Teachers and volunteers helped, and Dad was in charge of the stores. The kiddies were sorted out, kitted out, and people came and collected them: they were all labelled, according. Lucky for us, some of them never turned up. They'd dropped out, I s'ppose, changed their minds, or their Mams had, so there was generally something left over: a nice little coat, a pair of socks, funny trousers down to the knees. It was all new stuff! I can see Brian now, he looked so smart, his gas mask in a little box on his back—he had six, two Mickey Mouses! He was growing and all, what with the chocolate and the sample cans Whickey let me have, and the extra eggs.

There was a good fairy about us; now and then there definitely was. Every night when I got home and before I went to the school I had to make the beds. I got up so early, you see, left the others sleeping, and our Mother hadn't got the strength any more. Well, this night I went upstairs as usual, and I was about to drop down on our bed, just for a minute before I started, just roll down into the valley there still smelling of last night's sleep, when I seen it. An *egg*! In the middle of the pillow—a golden-brown egg.

I picked it up: it was a real egg, warm, perfect. I thought: E's playin a game with me! The next night when I went up—there was another egg! But Brian said 'No!' He hadn't been up! I didn't tell our Mother in case it *was* him. I couldn't a-stood to see her lamming him. Else said she had done, once. He was running round and round the table

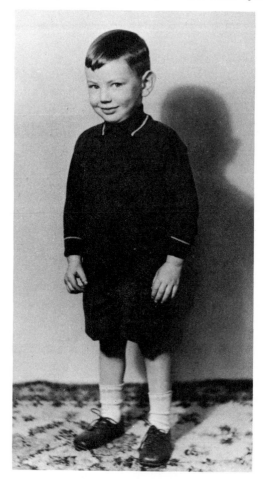

Brian

and it got on our Mother's nerves. Else told me: 'I wanted to 'it *er!*'
By the end of the week I'd collected six eggs.

Now as I said, our bed, Brian's and mine, it was a single bed,
pushed up against a tiny casement. On the seventh day, Sunday, I
kept watch. Lo and behold, late afternoon, up the slate roof comes
one of our Mother's hens—she was a Rhode Island Red—so stately,
squeezes through the casement. I left it open for airing, well, just
enough to let a bit of air in; how she got through I'll never know. She
plonked herself down on the pillow—and laid an egg! I could hardly

believe my eyes! How proud she was! The clucks! I laughed out loud, clapped my hands.

'Brian! Mam! Come quick! 'Ave a look at this!'
She sat there so regal, looking at us from the pillow.
'*Just in time!*' said our Mother. 'That's why the bugger weren't layin!'
Brian had the eggs. Our Mother looked on them as *extra*, so he was having an egg most days! He was growing; you couldn't tell he was an early child, hardly.

*

New Year's Day at the Canning Bob came up and said something to me. I think it was 'Happy New Year!' I smiled. Well, I was happy. I know I had to leave Brian, but he loved our Mother and Dad; sometimes I thought he got on better with them than he did with me. I was oiling the machine that you put the cans in for the syrup. It was going round. I had to do some jobs with the machines running, see, and the oil can—well, you could get the spout caught if you weren't quick. You'd got to be *quick*. It was a heavy machine. I smiled at Bob. Yes, I was happy! My thumb went in. It was in the cogs.

I might have screamed; I think I did. The only thing I can remember clearly is Bob's face—*white*. I was taken to the nurse at the Alum, but they had to take me to hospital in the end so that just wasted time. The blood! They couldn't stitch it, cos it was so mauled. There was nowhere to stitch!

Three months it took, to try to put my thumb right. There should have been a notice saying: '*Don't touch the machines when they're going.*' There wasn't. I didn't get any compensation. I was paid my wages, but now I think I should a-got something. It's a disfigurement—*look*! And when I went back to the Canning I wasn't with Bob any more.

''Ave you 'eard?' said Ethel.
'On that bloody machine?'
It was a sore point with me. When I came back Whickey put me on the potato machine. I think he was annoyed cos I'd been away for so long, and I'd been handy for him. It was dreadful, the potato machine: scalding water splashing over your legs, even through trousers. I have the scars still. He'd got a new girlfriend—independently.
Gladys came crying to me. 'E wants to be near er,' she said. 'E just

stands on the slippery slope'—that's what we called it—'pretends to be lookin at us.'

Well, all the tables faced him.

'Straight from *school*!'

'Yes,' I said, 'what a pickle.'

We both knew it was all over, but Gladys kept hoping . . . I couldn't think of anything to say, to cheer her up.

The new girlfriend had quite a hard job, actually. She had to *bend* all day, put the tins o' taters in the machine Bob 'n' me had made, to

'We all had to turn out.' Stratford-upon-Avon Produce Canners Ltd, Second World War (Mary sitting, second row, fifth from right)

lacquer them. Gladys was right. There was prettier, better girls he could have had, the Harrises for example, they came on bikes, they had *green* boiler suits, I don't know why. I had a blue one, a boy's, cos I was so thin, but the Harrises were glamour girls, and Mrs Whickey was ever so pretty. So was Gladys.

There was nothing I could do to help her. She was crying all the time.

'*Er*! What's e want with *er*?'

And I used to pass it all on to Ethel. I was a sneak.

Ethel said: 'Why don't you ask for a move? Get your old job back?

I could put a word in. Nobody can do it like you! Bob says so, all the time. You should 'ear what e says 'bout you.'

'No.'

I think it was my pride. I was frightened things wouldn't be the same, that I wouldn't be able to do it, with my hand.

'Any road,' I said, 'what'm I s'pposed to 'ave 'eard?'

'We've gotta 'ave our *photograph* took! Whickey wants a *photograph*—of er!'

'Poor Gladys!'

So we all had to turn out, the whole Canning. And there she is still, so meek 'n' mild, and there's us, and there's the Director, he wasn't in the know but it was slowly dawning . . . You can see his expression. That young boy, he was called up, after. He went and got killed; his name was Jackie Boyce. Whickey put all the glamour in the front row; that was typical, always one eye on the future. But Ethel was right. This time he'd met his Waterloo.

He got sent to Africa! *Af-ri-ca*! She went with him—to a canning factory in the middle of the jungle. He was the nicest boss I ever had, Whickey, and that's what happened to him.

Chapter Eighteen

I told you I would always avoid opening a front door. Our Mother had a lot of warnings: don't pass on the stairs, whatever you do don't cross the knives! If you spill the salt chuck some over your left shoulder, quick. Her favourite one was: Never look at the new moon through glass! She went spare if one of us did that. Dad used to have to go outside, tell her if it was shining.

'Yes,' he said, 'it is.'

Then she said: 'Don't look out the winder, there's a new moon.'

'What about me glasses Mam? When I goes out?'

'Spectacles don't count.'

But opening a door! That was my own private dread. The door to the school house had four arched panes, like four church windows, with frosted glass. Through them you could see shapes in the porch, against the light. I could tell if it was gypsies, they were very distinctive: a big basket, shoulders out to bear the weight, like this, not tall . . . 'The gypsies'll fetch you!' But today . . . my heart turned over. It wasn't gypsies, but there was no mistaking.

I let our Mother go. I sat tight at the bottom of the stairs, with Brian. There was a long passage at the school house, from the front door right to the stairs. We were playing with a ball. We got plenty of rubber balls from the playground; they sailed over the wall, got stuck in our guttering. Bert climbed on the roof for them. I went on playing with the ball, but my heart was thumping too.

'Well,' our Mother was saying, 'I'll leave you two together.'

'Oh Sis,' I said. I had a little cry.

She put her arm round me. She said, 'Don't fret, love. E was a bastard, most of em are.' She laughed. 'Trouble is, e *was* different. You couldn't 'elp likin im.'

'Yes,' I said, 'just my bloody luck.'

'D'you *remember* . . . d'you remember ow you did cartwheels, top

93

of our road and e was goin by on is bike and—e was always on 'is own.'

That was true! He was. Sis remembering annoyed me.

'E was always alone,' she said, 'I reckon e just wanted to join in.'

'Well e did do didn't e?'

It's hard to explain, but I was still a bit jealous of Sis.

Later she said, 'I've come back from Coventry for good, Mary. I'm goin to start to en*joy* myself.'

I was shocked; I'd no idea she hadn't been doing! Although she was laughing she was very upset about something, I could tell. All my jealousy went.

'Oh Sis!'

It was such a comfort to know . . . Well, I'd always dreaded Sis, what she was going to say. And here she was! She saw Brian and she never said a word. She just said, 'Don't fret.'

'You never had un then, Sis?'

'No. But I might do now I see what a lovely lad *you* got . . .'

She was kindness itself. We both had a little cry and a laugh.

That wasn't the only knock on the door gave me a turn! The next came six o'clock in the morning! I was the only one up. I was creeping downstairs with a candle . . . and the door starts to open. The front door! Oh my God! I thought, Dad forgot to lock up! I heard a voice: 'It's only *Boll*rus!'

I froze.

'Don't be frightened—I got summat *for* you!'

'Course, I was frit to death. I ran back up the stairs, grabbed Brian. That was my first instinct, always.

It was our Jim's mate, Bollrus Chamberlain, and he wasn't half laughing at me! He'd brought a cheese, big as a full moon, the biggest cheese I'd ever seen—at that time of the morning!

'Jim says, "Ask no questions 'n' you'll be told . . ."'

I was thinking: What our Ede ud do for a piece o' this! She was worse'n a mouse for cheese!

Afterwards I saw him up the town.

He laughed and said, 'It's only *Boll*rus!' He does still, to this day.

I said: 'Yes, you bugger!'

I thought: It broke my dream, that cheese!

'Ey weren't it big! Where d'you find it?'

He just laughed.

We had a bit ourselves. Some went to a hotel. The rest was sold to a farmer from Snitterfield who handled stuff people had found, or couldn't manage.

*

Then I got a parcel. Everything was coming at once, and every time, it wasn't, you know, what I was expecting. I was waiting, hoping, for *some*thing. I couldn't put it behind me, like Sis.

She said, 'The past is past. Don't sit forever on an addled egg, Mary. There's plenty of fresh uns about! Forget it!'

I thought: I can't!

The postman said: 'There's a parcel from India, Mary, and you've gotta pay duty on it.'

I said: 'I don't know anybody in India!'

I didn't, but I had a wild thought . . .

'Well, you gotta pay if you wants it. Look—MISS MARY HEWINS— SCHOOL HOUSE— ALCESTER ROAD— STRATFORD-ON-AVON— ENGLAND.'

I paid him. I'd come over all queer, looking at that hand. It wasn't our Cyril's; I didn't know it. A little voice said: 'It's *im*! *E*'s in India! *E*'s sent you a present!'

I daren't open it. I put it on the table, sat staring at it. I pictured him in India, fighting the . . . who *was* they fighting? I got all my courage together and opened it. There were some lovely scarves inside!

'Oh!' I cried, 'Mam! Come an look! Ain't they lovely?'

Silk scarves, all colours of the rainbow!

'See *this*!'

I unfolded it once, twice, three times. It was all colours—mauve, red, brilliant blue—the colours gypsies like, lovely, light as air. You could a-drawn it through a key-hole. But what it *was*—I couldn't make that out. I tried it as a shawl. I put it over my head.

Our Mother said, very firm: 'It's a tablecloth.' You could see she loved it. 'Oo's it from?'

I looked again and found a note. 'WITH KIND REGARDS DONT FORGET ME WILL YOU REMEMBER THE ROOBAB— NORMAN.'

Norman?

'It'll be Norman Windsor,' said our Mother, 'well ain't that nice of him?' She looked at me as if to say: 'Is there anything between you two?'

I said: 'You can 'ave the tablecloth, Mam.'

How could I tell her how disappointed I was; how could I tell anybody?

Just to rub salt in she said: 'Norman must a-spent 'is last bit o' pay on this stuff! What does e mean: "*roobab*"?'

'I dunno.'

I didn't. I might a-done, once, but I'd forgot.

It was then I caught sight of her leaning across the chair. Her features were twisted into a face I didn't recognize.

Dad said: 'Your Mam can't *manage* any more.'

So I left work to look after her. She was in terrible pain, yes she was. The rupture was as big as that. When she sat down water came away; we had to pad her up. They said it would cost twenty pounds, the operation. We hadn't got it.

The doctor said: 'You should 'ave the operation—quick!' He said: 'If she 'as it she'll be perfect. It could be done easy.'

'Thank you, I shan't bother,' she said.

She didn't mind; she didn't want to be cut. I think she was frightened.

The doctor said: 'It's nothing!' but she wouldn't have it done.

I said: 'We'll get the money.'

Then she started falling down in the street; she was overweight, our Mother, a heavy woman, yet she never used to eat *any*thing! All she used to do was sit about, didn't go to bed, drink pop for her indigestion, and belch and belch.

Brian would run in and say: 'Can I 'ave a drink o' pop, Granny?'

'Well,' she said, 'that's all I got—but you can 'ave it.'

She didn't *bother* any more. Brian just had a bun for his dinner, or a glass o' pop. As I said, Marg did the washing, and our Ede, she was ever so good. Our Mother didn't even do the baking no more; Dad cooked the dinner. He worked damned hard. He still did the Dragon every night, collected the glasses, mopped up the beer and stuff, gave them a song when they wanted. And every morning after the fires he went back to the Dragon, to scrub. I did the rest of the school.

She couldn't do nothing. She just used to sit, dig that little bone into her apple, and eat it, like this. It was hollow, and as she scooped it filled with apple. Then she sucked.

I thought: She's old! Our Mother's old!

I wouldn't let myself think any further. It was kept locked up, in the cellar of my mind: the biggest fear of all.

*

Marg said: 'I'll take Brian off your 'ands today, Mary, take im out your way.'

They were so late coming back! I kept looking at the clock. I started to go frantic, I thought he'd been kidnapped. When they came . . .

'Ohh!'

She'd stuck his little mouth up to stop the bleeding, stuffed it with cotton wool. His teeth had gone through his lip.

She said: 'E's 'ad an accident.'

You never seen such a face in your life! I screamed!

'Why didn't you get *doctor* Marg?'

I got him to the surgery, I don't know how—I was nearly out of my mind. I thought: Oh God! 'Is looks is ruined!

What I called Marg! It seemed her Daphne had tied Brian's little trike to her two wheeler, and started to pedal away and hit a stone . . .

I said to the doctor: 'Will it 'urt 'is other teeth?'

He didn't get them for ever such a long time. The others went blue and then they dropped out. I thought when he didn't get teeth: Oh God! E ain't goin to get none! But he did. There was only the tiniest scar.

The doctor said: 'You should get your Mother to 'ave the operation. It'll kill er else.'

He was getting exasperated, you could see.

*

She said, 'There's somebody's brought flowers round.'

'*Flowers?*'

'That chap from Canning.'

I thought: Oh it's Bob.

'What's e want? Bringin you flowers? It's not *you* 'ad the accident —*this* time.' Our Mother said: 'I didn't ask im in.'

She would never let in anyone as a rule, especially chaps. She would never let me go out at night without Brian. If she so much as seen me talking to a chap . . .

'I 'spect e's got a conscience.'

I was going to say it weren't Bob's fault, my hand, then I thought: What's the point?

'Bloody should 'ave. *Flowers!* Any road,' she said, 'I've chucked em out. Lilac.'

Our Mother was that superstitious! What was the point in argu-

ing? She was in a funny mood these days, distracted. Sometimes I
thought . . .

She said: 'Cyril says its very hot.'

She'd had a letter. Our Cyril was in Yugoslavia; we didn't know
that then, o' course, but 'hot' was the code. It meant hot fighting.

Chapter Nineteen

I couldn't understand the war, really. You know, what it was really *for*—'cept we was winning now, and the Germans and the Italians and the Japs was on the other side. I *liked* the Germans—there, I've said it! I wouldn't a-said so, aloud, then, but I felt sorry for them. Oh and they were handsome, a lot of the German prisoners, fair hair, bright cheeks, only young chaps. They had a look reminded me . . . Early on in the war a German plane had gone over the school. I was at work, but our Mother was there, she was out feeding the hens and she said: 'I never seen a sight like it! E *waved*! To the kiddies—and me!' She said: 'The cheeky devil! The cheeky bugger! 'Ad the nerve to wave!' But she was laughing, as she remembered it.

They used to wave to *me* and all, as they went up the Alcester Road in lorries, back to their camp. They'd been working all day on the fields and farms. They waved and laughed. I think they were happy to be caught. I used to think: I wonder if *e's* a prisoner somewhere? I wonder if *e's* waving from a lorry, glad to be caught and out of the war? Somehow I never could imagine him caught. The more I wondered about it the more I thought: No, e'd a-took a risk and won a medal or bin blown to bits. That was his style.

I liked the Germans much more'n the Italians. *They* were so dark, the Italian prisoners, and all over the place, especially at the pictures. When Brian and me went to the pictures—there was nowhere else to go, see, I used to take him always, Sunday nights, well I had to, our Mother made me, unless it was an English film—it was crowded with Italians! There were hundreds of them in the queue. One queue went right from the picture house, right round, round the corner, past the Dragon and along Arden Street. That was the dear queue. We used to go in the other one, on the cheap side: up and round by Fox's back.

When we got in we had a job to get a *seat*! They were near the front, the cheap ones, and I always tried to get about four rows from the front. I was quick: you had to be! The Italians filled them mostly. Sometimes you could say that having to take Brian everywhere was a handicap—but not with them! They came over and gave us sweets, big round glassy sweets, all colours. They lasted ages. The Italians had packs and packs of them. One showed us a lighter he'd made from scrap: shaped like a miniature pistol, so clever, every detail. He thought we might buy it, I 'spect. Some hopes! Oh how Brian longed and longed for that lighter! He never said, he never was a *grabby* lad, he just looked and I sensed how he longed for it.

Cyril in Italy

The funny thing was, the Italians were so quiet. They all seemed to be on their own, even in a crowd, not mix with one another, no jabbering.

I whispered to Brian: 'Save the rest for Uncle Cyril!' and: 'Stop lookin at em!'

They used to gaze at him, sort of fierce, sad. They gave him some peculiar stares. They were so dark, rough, like tramps, or gypsies. I thought they might kidnap him. The world was mad! Upside down! Somewhere in Italy—we knowed our Cyril was in Italy now—there could a-been a woman wondering 'bout *him*: Why's e lookin at my kiddie like that? What's e thinkin, this foreign man? I didn't fancy them at all.

I had a picture in my mind's eye of Cyril sat in a cottage in Italy. We'd had a letter; it said, '*It's all olive oil, Mam!*'

'My poor babby!'

Our Cyril had gone from being a man to a boy to a babby! I thought: E'll soon be back in the bloomin womb!

He said: '*I sit at the table with the family. Its like ome hear. They pass the wine round and theirs the kiddies and the wenches. Tell Jim the wenches is v. glamorus.*'

That upset our Jim, o' course! Cyril loved to tease. He seemed to have been half way round the world: Africa, Yugoslavia, Italy. He was a bloody war hero, really.

Cyril said: '*I turned down the stripes.*'

Dad laughed. 'I did and all,' he said, 'in 'fifteen!'

'That's nothin to be proud of!'

But you could see she didn't mind *any*thing as long as Cyril was alive. We all felt the same. The relief! He asked us to send chocolate and tea and sugar. He'd got some racket going.

I thought: I wonder if e's started card parties?

And so everything we had went to Italy, 'cept milk chocolate: the Bourneville with the red label, our rations, the lot.

'*Send more chocs, and sweets,*' he said, '*and TEA.*'

We could get sugar from the brewery. Tea was the biggest challenge. Our Mother went to the Maypole, saw a woman there; she exchanged little bits of jewellry for tea. That's where those earrings went that Dad found—she'd loved them so, long ear bobs, brass but they polished up like gold. He'd found them, cleaning. I see that woman sometimes in Stratford and I think: I wonder where those ear bobs are now?

The Italians couldn't understand the film: they didn't speak the language. They watched anything, just like me. Well, *almost*! As I said, I wouldn't watch English films. I drew the line there. The actors all talked as if they'd got plums in their mouths, you couldn't tell what they were saying—the *words*!—and they was always black and white. We saw every American film that came to the picture house.

We went Sunday nights, in the shillings; the back row was one and nine. We didn't go Sat'days cos it was so rough, then. We could hear it from the school. There'd be trouble at the Dragon—a dreadful commotion—then, all of a sudden, whistles! The military police was there! Red caps jumping out of army wagons. There was different regiments, you see, at Long Marston camp; the way back was by train. They all called at the Dragon: the Pioneers, the Engineers, the RAF from Snitterfield, the Canadians. They all went to the pub on their way back to camp. There were big fights. We couldn't get to sleep for hours sometimes.

Sat'day night Dad was in the Dragon singing. When things got nasty he got under the counter, quick. He worked all the time; how the hell he did it I do not know. Pub work was terrible hard in those days: filthy boots, spit, sick . . . Some nights he got coupons, for Brian's clothes, or he brought back chewing-gum. He cadged chewing-gum and fags off the Yanks; there was suddenly a lot of them about town. They loved his singing; they couldn't get enough of it.

Those old songs—where'd he picked them up? Once upon a time I knowed them all, inside out. He used to sing as we did the school, filled the coal buckets, shifted the desks.

'On the top of 'is tombstone
You'll find these lines written:
'Now all you young men
Take warnin from me,
And never go courtin
Along wi the flash girls
For the flash girls of the city
Was the ruin of me.'

Chapter Twenty

The noise of the horns woke me. Well, they didn't *wake* me, I think I was still asleep when I went to the window and looked out and saw the soldiers. There they were, waving from the biggest trucks you ever seen, and the one parked opposite the school had a great long nose with a star on top. *Yanks*! I don't know if they was beckoning *me*, they seemed to be doing: sirens going, horns, men laughing and shouting.

'Come on!' they shouted, '*come on*!'

They seemed to be shouting 'Come on, Mary!'

I took Brian in my arms, our Mother and Dad was sleeping, it was two o'clock. Blackie? He weren't about, lucky for me, he was out on the prowl somewhere.

There was a big moon that night, there must a-been. *Some*thing lit up the yard from the school house to the main road. Brian's face was a picture; he was more awake'n me.

'Shhh!' I said, 'your Granny'll 'ave a fit if she finds out!'

I was only in my nightgown and a blanket; he had pyjamas on.

'It's Victory!' the Yanks said. 'Hurry!'

And they hauled us into the back of one of the trucks. It was like a cattle truck, with rails round, full o' folks already, folks from Stratford. You sensed they was there, aside of you, but you *felt* you was alone, all alone as we thundered down Grove Road, bumped over the level crossing, past the Salmon Tail, towards the cemetery. The Yanks kept sounding the horns, sang songs I'd never heard before, songs about America.

'Look at the lights!' I said to Brian.

Lights were coming on in houses all along the Evesham Road. People could hear the din, wondered what was going on I 'spect. Nobody had to draw their curtains now. We left the town behind. Right to the top of Bordon Hill we went, right to the top. Did you know that's where they found star stones, once, Bordon Hill? Dad told us. Little stars that dropped to earth and turned to stone. Somebody gave me a fag and I could see Brian's face all lit up with excitement. It *was* exciting. You felt like shouting: 'I'm the King of the Castle!'

Stratford was down there, miles and miles away. It was like a dream; it *was* a dream! And the Yanks swung round on the top of Bordon Hill, swung those great big trucks round, in the middle of the road there, and down to earth we started to come, tearing down, horns blaring. *Vroom!*

'Thank you,' I said, 'say "thank you" Brian,' but they didn't hear.

'Come to the White Swan!' they cried. That was the Red Cross Club.

'I daren't.'

They didn't press me—they didn't have to! Past the corner by the school we went: did I feel guilty! I wondered what our Mother would say if she woke and found us gone, but that didn't stop me. It was all dark at the school house, quiet as the grave. Good! I thought.

'Mary Mary Quite Contrary!'

I smiled when they called me that. There was one G.I., he was a joker, he'd started calling me that. He found out my name was Mary. He came from Hollywood, he said.

'Pull the other one!'

'It's the truth! It's a real place!'

He wanted my address. I shook my head and laughed. I knew one or two girls who'd started going with the Yanks. I liked their films— but he was right, I *was* contrary! I have a contrary nature. Perhaps I take after our Mother, I don't know.

'I never thought of gettin 'ome,' he said. 'I gave my lighter to a gal in London, or I'd a-give it you! You've gotta smile'd make the flowers come out. This your brother?'

Brian gave him a look.

'We're goin to 'ave a bonfire, sonny,' he said, 'you bet we are.'

When we got to the White Swan they ran inside and came out with a pianna. A pianna! They pushed it into the road, by the Fountain there, had a bit of a play and a sing-song, then two more Yanks came running out with bits o' furniture, it was all they could find to burn, I s'ppose, and whoosh! They bust into flames and everybody was laughing and shouting 'Victory!'

If you had asked me then, 'Did it really happen?', I would a-said 'No'. But it did, cos my nightgown was covered with oil, I never could get it off. And when I woke at six, to start work, there was Brian fast asleep aside of me, clutching a stick of gum.

*

Our Mother must a-known. When I was getting dressed, I went like a mouse always, so's not to disturb them, but she must a-heard me and she said: 'Cyril'll be comin home!'

That, I thought, is a mixed blessing. Dad was thinking the same, cos when she said, 'We'll let the fireworks off tonight, George!'—she was so excited!—he said, 'You can. *I'm* not!'

'It's Victory!'

'I'm not lettin those buggers off,' he said.

I'd never seen a fireworks show, and those fireworks was *whoppers*: like sticks o' dynamite, V-2 rockets, that long, bulging with gunpowder! One morning there they were—in the porch. Dad hadn't wanted to keep them; he was frit of fire, I don't know why. Every night he doused the fires at the school with water, tipped the ashes on the garden, still sizzling.

'I'm not 'avin em in 'ere,' he said, 'we'll give em back.'

But we didn't know *who'd* left them, we couldn't give them back, and we daren't dump them anywhere cos of the fire risk. So Dad got a pan: it was a great big crock pan, earthenware—we made wine in it. He cussed! 'Shells!' he said, 'bleedin shells!' He stacked them in the pan, in the cellar. And every night he crept out with this great big pan with the fireworks in it, and let it down over the wall by the school, 'to tek the blast,' he said. Every night he did that, when he'd put the fires out.

'We gotta let em off *some* time,' said our Mother.

'I'm not advertisin.'

'That's what they're for.'

'And 'ave all the coppers in the neighbourhood come round, sniffin about?'

'What *we* got to hide?'

Well! What we'd got in our cellar besides fireworks was *nobody's* business; our Mother knowed that as well as Dad. But she was desperate for a show, a celebration. We all was, really. Brian joined in: 'Go on Grandad!'

Dad stuck his ground. 'I'm not lettin off no shells, nor flares, fireworks, call em what you like—*ever*,' he said.

Our Mother went quiet. That afternoon after tea she sent word to

the brewery, to our Jim. The message came back: 'We'll 'ave the best display they ever seen in Stratford!'
We *did*.

It was in the school yard. Jim came and set them up in the school yard, by the road. There was a lot of fumbling about with matches, and Jim trying to read the instructions: 'What does it *say*, our Mary?' Then all at once the world really did go mad! There was green and red explosions, rockets bust in the sky, and scores of parachutes came floating down. We had Catherine wheels going berserk on the gates there, the boys' and girls' gates, and a bloke with a big 'V' sign who Jim started off at the wrong end. There was burning rocket cases all over the place. They went out with little *phuts*! made me scream and jump. It was more like war'n peace!

Our Mother said: 'E'll set the school on fire!' and 'Your Dad was right!' You could see she was enjoying herself. 'E's gone balmy!' she said.

The smell! It was an exciting smell, burning black, hot, it went to your brain. It reminded me . . . Then another load of rockets went up: swoosh, bang, *ohhhh*!

All the people on their way to the station had stopped dead in their tracks, you can imagine, and the soldiers, Yanks, everybody! Nurses and patients came out of the hospital, to gawp. The Dragon had no customers. Crowds of folks sat on the wall, pushing and cheering, egging us on. 'Let's 'ave another o' *those*, Jim!' They were beautiful fireworks, beautiful. Nobody had ever seen anything like them.

Our Jim started showing off. 'Now you've *all* gotta chance of seein this spectacular display!' he said, 'no charge! Not just the C.O.'s and the toffs!'

They'd been heading for the top brass, for a private party, bound to be. That's what our Jim reckoned. Well, he could a-been right. The people cheered and cheered. Jim fancied himself as Robin Hood.

❧

We never heard from the police. That was a wonder: they must have known about it, they must have seen it! All Stratford seen that firework display and Jim spoke the truth there: it was spectacular. All except Dad. He'd gone missing; we never found him. Brian went down in the morning and there he was, hiding in the cellar; he brought him back.

'They've gone,' Brian said, 's'alright!'

He'd had a lovely time—well for a little kiddie those fireworks was magic! But even at that age he had patience with the old man, drunk or sober, more'n I had, I'll admit it. Well, I don't have to tell you, I couldn't stick him. He and Brian *got on*. When he started chunnering 'bout rats—there were rat holes all over the school, inside the classrooms, the partitions, there was one old rat with grey whiskers, a great big thing, *King Rat* by the looks on him, he was too crafty for the rat catcher—Brian said: 'I'll learn Blackie to catch em Grandad!'

Some hopes of that! Blackie had been hiding down there, and all!

Street party (Wellesbourne Grove, Stratford-upon-Avon) to celebrate Victory, 1945: Emma standing to left of table, in big hat, Brian just in front of her

The next night Jim came round again. Hullo, I thought, another blooming card party, and guess oo'll 'ave to clean up after em! But he came on his own to talk to our Mother, and his voice was grim. I was under the teacher's desk, getting up the rubbish. That basket was big enough to take three footballs, but Miss Farmer couldn't aim a ball o' *hair* in straight, at twelve inches! Sometimes I reckoned she did it a-purpose.

I heard Jim say: 'Arch told me. E was there, the bastard. Arch wouldn't make a mistake. It was *im*! Watchin our bloody fireworks!'

Our Mother said something I couldn't catch.

He was always trying to impress her. It was no good; Cyril was the favourite there, always.

'This time I'll 'ave the bugger. E'll never do that to no-one, never again.'

It was *him*! It must be! He'd come back! My stomach turned over. He'd been there, at the fireworks, he could a-been near us, touching. I'd thought . . . maybe . . . I felt a real pain, here. I thought, 'E's come back to Stratford. E's alright! E got through the war.'

Chapter Twenty-one

'There's a letter,' our Mother said, 'for Brian. It took long enough to get 'ere.'

For Brian?

'Ah,' she said, 'I opened it.'

The tears welled up in her eyes, started to stream down her face, you know, like a spring in a field—have you ever found one? The astonishment! I'd never seen her cry before, not like that. I was so astonished.

Brian said: 'I'll read it for you, Granny.'

He was crying too, practically, cos she was. But the writing was joined up; he couldn't manage. I wanted to say to her: 'Please don't cry, *please*!' I couldn't bear to see her cry.

Bert came in and he read it:

Dear Brian,

Well I'm in Germany now and it ain't much good out here their is 'nix in the winkle' and the people are none too good so I'm planning to get out as quickly as possible.

Be a good lad and remember me to your Mother, Granny, Grandad, and Bert, and I'm hoping to get my ticket next year, and then I shall stay at home for good 'I hope' so I will wish you Goodnight and God Bless you and don't forget to be a good lad, Cheerio,

Uncle Cyril
Gunner C. Hewins

'Oh,' said our Mother, 'I can die happy now.'

What had Cyril ever done to deserve so much love? How to explain it? You could see Dad thinking the same. For the first time, just for a minute, I was on his side, not hers.

*

Brian was seven years old. It was getting to be a squash in that single bed. And Blackie! I'd worked out he was over a hundred, in human years.

I thought: 'Ere's me in my bloody prime sleepin with a kiddie and a hundred year ole chap!

I was restless, counting and doing. You know, I was even counting the times a spider went across the ceiling, back'ards and for'ards, back'ards and for'ards. Blackberrying time came and went, the first Mop after the war, the first winter, the first spring, soon it would be summer. I sat looking at the ladies in the fireplace, no fire now; they didn't seem so pretty. I didn't want to go to bed; I couldn't sleep. I lay awake, tossing and turning. It was so cold, so hot! I'd got so's I was watching everywhere: watching for *him*. I thought: If I see im, just once, I'll know! I'll know e's *alive*!

You see, a dreadful idea had come into my mind. It was like being on the very edge of Bird's Pit, the pit that was flooded, nobody knew how deep or what was at the bottom yet all the time you wanted to go closer 'n' closer, have a look, find out . . .

Our Mother came to tuck Brian in. She always tucked him in, gave him a big kiss. But this night she said: 'Ow should you like to go up to London duck, to see the King 'n' Queen? You and your Mam? The day after tommorrer?'

*

We hadn't a clue what to do. We were lost—on Paddington Station! It was eleven o'clock: three hours late! We had to stand in the train, all the way. The crowds! It was a wonder we'd got so far. All the world seemed to be going to London. It was like being lost at the Mop. I was once, when I was a little kiddie. I can still feel the panic: I'd let go our Ede's hand.

There was no chance of finding Ern—he was s'pposed to be meeting us—no chance even of *seeing* him! I hung on to Brian for grim death; Gwen grabbed my coat. It was the blind leading the blind. She'd wanted to come. Else asked me: 'Will you take Gwendoline? She wants to see the Queen.' So I said 'Yes.'

'Look!' said Brian.

Flo had written: 'You catch an 88 bus.' He'd spotted a sign with '*88*' on it! We went and stood by it, and all of a sudden these Londoners, these Cockneys—well, we didn't realize they was in a queue—started shouting: 'You bleedin well get to the back!'

It was the last bus! '*Last bus!*' the conductress shouted, and there we were—stranded.

Our case was full of brown sugar; it weighed a ton. My feet hurt. I kept thinking of that doctor's words: 'Oo wears them shoes? Er'll be a cripple afore she's thirty!'

Gwen was crying, I was tearful. Well, I didn't know what to do. Some kiddies ran up: 'Carry yer bags miss? Carry yer bags?' I clung tight to it, I can tell you, and to Brian's hand. No fear, I thought. They kept running alongside of us.

'No!' I said, '*no!*'

And then Brian spotted the taxi. He never hesitated. He ran into the middle of the road—and it stopped!

'Millais Buildings!' he said, he'd got it from the films, what to do, and we piled in.

I was thinking: Oh my God what's it goin to cost? It'll take all our money!

I opened the case; I'd hid my purse in it. One of the bags of sugar had bust. There was only three pound notes.

'Oh God,' I said aloud.

That started Gwen off again. On and on went that taxi, on and on.

It's goin to cost a fortune! I thought.

Outside we could see a *river*: black and glittery and oily, half a mile wide by the looks on it, at least, you couldn't see the other bank. Horrible. And just then he stopped, outside some toilets, all brown tiles, dark brown tiles. I was frit to death.

I thought: E's goin to do us in!

'That's a pound missus,' he said.

I gave it him, quick, and we jumped out like three field mice with the cat just behind. From the darkness came *Ern*! He'd waited at Paddington, waited and waited; then he thought we weren't coming.

'Ow much did e charge?'

Gwen and me was speechless! Brian told him.

'The bugger!'

The taxi driver had overcharged us. I didn't care: we'd *got there*!

So this was Millais Buildings! We couldn't believe it: brown tiles and concrete steps going up and up! Inside—oh were we glad to get inside—there was Flo and it was just like the old days. The first thing she did, before we'd got our coats off even, was count the sugar bags, weigh them. You could *hear* her brain ticking over. I thought: That's the last I'll see of them—or the results! Then she said: 'You've just come too late, our Mary! I've just 'ad to finish off the last of a bunch of *bananas*!'

Gwen's face fell, and Brian's. I'd told him about bananas. Our Flo had always *just* ate a bunch of bananas or a tin of chewing gum or a six pound walnut cake. She counted everything, weighed it up—and it had always gone, just before you arrived!

In the morning—we'd brought some bread and bacon with us, *food supplies*—I opened the window and chucked the rinds out, cos I did that at home, for the fowl.

Flo said: 'Christ, our Mary, they'll 'ave you up!'

And when I looked out, really looked out, I saw that we were high up, in the sky. I'd forgot about all those stairs, last night. There weren't no fowl. I was staring at rows and rows of wounded men, all wounded men, heads bandaged in white, legs up in the air. Two of them started waving and shouting; well, I'd only got my nightgown on. I shut the window—quick! It gave me a turn; it was a sight I wasn't expecting.

'They're officers. It's a hospital for officers,' said Flo. *'Toffs.'*

Then she had a row with Ern; she showed off. The result was, she said she wouldn't come with us to the Parade.

'I'll find my own way,' she said.

The rest of us sat on the Tate Gallery steps: Ern and me and Brian and Gwen and Flo's two boys; Teddy who'd won a scholarship to Westminster School, he was very brainy; and Jimmy. We had this good spot on the steps, *reserved*, cos our Flo worked at the Tate, cleaned it.

What's she up to? I wondered. Where's our Flo gone?

There was no sign of her.

'Where's the *Queen*?' said Gwen.

The Parade went past the steps, all the old generals and that, they were in big shiny cars, past the bottom of the steps, along the Embankment.

I remember thinking: E's only a little bloke, no bigger'n Dad!

Brian liked the army vehicles going past.

'Where's the Queen?' said Gwen.

There was somebody quite well-to-do at the Tate, must a-been, cos everybody in the Parade seemed to turn their heads and look at *us*!

The Rowes cheered and cheered, clapped like mad. We just gawped. Cockneys are different, aren't they? The war had been bad for them; they were there, all through the bombing, in the shadow of Big Ben, practically. Can you imagine? Flo told me: 'We watched

em comin, up the river in the moonlight. Like shoals o' mackerel.'
And she'd been frit of *thunder*! Flo was always one step ahead of
the rest of us.

There was no sign of her at the Parade. But when we got to Millais
Buildings she was there before us and she said:

'You should a-come with *me*, our Mary!'

She'd found a ten-bob note!

What with the Parade, and panicking, and worrying about how
long our money would last, I never had any time to think. That's
what our Mother had had in mind, I 'spect. When she sent word I
could come back I only thought, 'Hooray!'

Flo was crying at the station. She said: 'You remember the last time
we was all together? We came to Stratford with Fred?'

How could I forget it?

'Our poor Jess,' she said.

'And Fred.'

Ern's brother young Fred was killed in the war.

Flo said: 'When me Dad seen me off he said, "Ta-ta, Flo!"' There
were tears in her eyes. 'When I got 'ome I said to Ern, "I *wished* I'd a-
give im summat. I do wish I'd a-give our Dad a drink."'

I smiled to myself. Yes, it was just like the old times, only Jess
wasn't there. Oh Jess, I thought, I still miss you.

Chapter Twenty-two

Stall at Stratford-upon-Avon Mop, 1940s

Dad and Brian tried and tried and tried to win a Lambeth boy.* It was threepence a go. They were all afternoon trying to win him, and then they came home from the Mop so disappointed. Lambeth boys had just come out. You had tickets, see, there were flashlights; it was a proper wangle.

After tea Dad said: 'Well Emm, I got sixpence. We're goin back to 'ave another go. I'm gonna *try*!'

She grumbled. 'You'll 'ave us in the workhus yet.'

But she never could resist wasting money on Brian either. She'd

* Large rag doll, presumably dressed as a coster.

spend her last pennies on a new toy for him. You could say Brian was the one thing they agreed on. Then she'd break into his money-box.

Blow me! Dad won the Lambeth boy! They came home with him! He had a little hat, velvety trousers and a dent in the back of his head. It was Dad's last sixpence and he got him for Brian. Praps he'd had a word with one of the moppers; most likely he did. He knowed a lot of them by name. They were a proper wangle, those stalls. The other thing they went to was the boxing booth.

Dad said: 'There's a young black chap in that booth fights like a wild cat. You seen nothin till you seen im.'

Brian brightened up—I don't know whether he *liked* the Lambeth boy really—and our Mother. She would never go to the booth at the Mop, but she always listened when Dad started to tell her about it. She listened to every word and there was a strange look in her eyes. Sometimes I thought: There's a whole half of her life I don't *know* about! That look came from there. I'd feel so jealous.

Brian said: 'I'm goin to be a boxer Gran!'

I thought: Over my dead body.

'E took me cap, after'ards, for the money! E borrowed me cap an e give Grandad a drink!' That wiped the smile off her face! 'E said: " 'Ere y'are, George, get yourself a drink!'

'Huh.'

'And there was a man. E kept followin us. Every time I turned round e was there.'

Dad said nothing. But he looked at our Mother, and she looked at me. I felt a sort of wild excitement. I hadn't felt that way for years.

I said to Brian, low: 'Us'll go back to Mop. Just the two of us, look for that man.'

*

It was the first proper Mop after the war. You never seen so many people, pushing and shoving, determined to get out, have a good time.

'There e is!' Brian shouted. To him it was a game.

A big chap had got on the cakewalk. He stumbled on, then he lost his grip. My heart turned over. He was drunk! His coat was coming off; gradually he slumped to the floor. There was something familiar . . . Everybody was screaming, but nobody heard, nobody realized. We couldn't take our eyes off him.

I thought: E'll *die*!

I started to run forwards and stopped. It was as if the cakewalk had took a *hold*—his whole body was shaking—as if something horrible had got inside of him. It was a nasty sight. We stared and stared, and in the end the Mop man realized. The shaking died down to a tremble; the whole cakewalk scrunched to a halt.

They sat him down on the steps. The grime and blood! His coat and shirt had been ripped open.

'It ain't 'im!' said Brian.

It wasn't.

'Come on,' I said. I wanted to get it out of my mind, that great big beer-filled stomach. I felt sick.

'Mam!' said Brian. He catched hold of my sleeve. I jumped! A deep voice was saying 'Ullo!'

'It ain't im, come on!' said Brian.

Another chap was leering down at me, said he'd been injured in the war. He was leering at Brian and all, summing up the situation, you could see.

'What 'bout meetin—later?' he said, 'when you've put the nipper to bed?'

'Come on Mam!'

Brian glared at him, tried to pull me away; well, I didn't need much pulling.

'It ain't im!' he said.

The game had gone sour, so had the Mop, even the sound of the organ, you know, *hellish*. The face of that tall man leered down at us.

I wanted to get home, fast. I never thought, I started back up Wood Street towards Rother Market, but hundreds of people was trying to do the same thing. I wanted to get home. Somebody panicked; kiddies screamed. They got wedged, us in the middle. Stalls started creaking, caving in.

I thought: If I faint we've 'ad it!

Brian said: 'This way Mam!'

We clambered over one of the stalls, and we got to safety.

*

I was never so pleased to see Sis in my life.

'Oh Sis!' I said; I dropped everything and threw my arms round her. How to explain? How to explain to anyone, even her?

'And ow's my little lad?'

I was washing Brian in the sink.

I said: 'E won a Lambeth boy yesterday!' I couldn't tell her the

Post-war Mop Fair, Stratford-upon-Avon: American Fountain towards left; behind it, White Swan Hotel

rest. She'd think I was balmy. I always washed him in the sink, his back and that. I remember Bert came by with a rabbit—the young chaps laid traps on the railway bank—cos he laughed and gave Brian a poke and said ' 'Ere's another Belsen victim!'

Brian's shoulder blades stuck out, he was dreadfully thin. We'd seen what the Germans had done on the news at the pictures: piles of bodies, mountains of them. Yes. You couldn't believe they could do such things, not those young lads on lorries, waving . . . I couldn't believe it. But it was *true*! We'd seen.

I said: 'Tek it away, it's orrible,' meaning the rabbit. I said: 'Ey Sis, you know that film . . . What's up?'

She said: 'Get ready for a shock. I seen im.'

'Oo?'

I knew before she said it, *who*.

'In the Horse 'n' Jockey'—she worked behind the bar there—'a while ago. I wasn't goin to tell you.'

'I don't want to know.'

''E came in bold as brass. I gave im a piece of my mind. I really let im 'ave it.'

I should have been grateful to her for sticking up for me, that's what friends are for, as Sis said, but all I could think was: Why don't she mind er own bloody business? Why don't they *all*?

'I told you Sis, I don't want to know.'

I dried Brian fast and I sent him off. Oh my heart! It was thumping. 'Let's go outside!' I said.

It was so bright, autumn. Yellow and gold. When you looked up through the lime trees by the school house that's all you could see: yellow and gold. I told myself: You can think of im without pain, now! It was just that awful thumping.

Sis said: 'Well I 'ope it was im!' She laughed. 'E's changed.'

I had a pain then, alright. I panicked. 'What d'ye mean, "changed"?'

''Is looks.'

No! I thought, not them! Anything but them!

'I wouldn't a-known im,' she said.

Was he wounded or what? You heard stories, 'bout airmen coming back all scarred, horrible, or a soldier with a leg off, and the girl giving them up and I always thought: I wouldn't! I'd still a-loved you! I pictured myself being all noble like the heroine and taking him on, horribly wounded, knocked about, when nobody else wanted him. Like those men at Flo's . . . *They* weren't real, though, they were far enough away not to be real: in the sky, far away. The day I'd bust in and seen Dad was real. I can see him still. And I knew I could never bear it, really. 'She can't stick er Dad!' It was him all over again. Our Mother would say when I was little: 'Go on, give your Dad a kiss!' I never would. The ugliness. I couldn't.

'What's up with im?' I hardly dared ask it: 'Is e spoilt?'

Sis frowned. I had to press her.

'Well . . . it was the most mysterious thing. E'd *dyed* . . .'

I felt, you know, as if a door had blowed open somewhere, in my mind. There was a cold draught.

'E'd . . . *dyed 'is hair*! And that's not all . . . E'd got a . . . a . . .'

'*Wot?*'

'Dyed 'is hair. *Black.*'

'It was beautiful, 'is hair. Like . . . Oh God!'

I started to laugh. Yes, I started to laugh, and Sis did, there under the lime trees outside the school house; leaning up against one of the lime trees I nearly bust my sides. It was as if I was free of a terrible load.

'Oh my God!'

I was floating like thistledown. I can't describe it. I was free of him.

'Why?' I said, '*why*, Sis?'

She was laughing so. She said: 'What a disguise! Your Jim was lookin for im.'

'So was I!' I could say it now.

'Well, e never catched im. Good job! Might a-come off in 'is 'and! The *colour*, I mean!'

We shrieked.

'Ey praps e's joined Theatre!'

'To be or not to be—*that* is the question!'

'E always was an actor.'

'*Starring*, tonight, in the Horse 'n' Jockey . . .'

'Oh Sis, ain't it marvellous?'

It was just like old times; we was altogether.

*

Our Mother looked at me sharpish when I came back in.

'What you bin up to?'

I ran upstairs. I sang as I tucked the sheets in, shoved the beds back.

> 'We'll take im to the churchyard
> We'll fire three volleys over im
> We'll play the Dead March
> As we carry im along . . .'

Even the idea of sharing with Cyril again couldn't dampen me.

> 'For e was a young soldier
> Oo's money I squandered
> E was a young soldier
> Cut down in 'is prime.'

'I've 'ad a bit o' good news,' I said when I came down.

'You look as if you lost a penny an found a pound.'

'I '*ave*!'

That's done it! I thought. Soon as I said it, I could have bit my tongue off. I thought she'd ask me for it 'just till Friday'. But she never.

'Hmm,' she said, 'London did you some good by the looks on it.'

Dad said: 'She can get on with *livin*. It's 'bout time.'

'Your idea of livin ain't mine. Nor ers.'

And that was the start of another row. I was in such a good mood I didn't mind, not like I usually did. I thought: Let them get on with it! I'm home.

Afterword

Porch, Church of England School buildings,
Stratford-upon-Avon (1983)

Only ghosts linger now in the porch, and dead leaves. No tramps call
for hot water: the workhouse has gone, and the Poor Laws. As for the
schoolchildren, they have been moved at last to modern premises.
There is sky where the bell once hung. Past the boys' and girls' gates

and over the railway bridge (no through trains from Stratford), traffic thunders relentlessly.

The little house beside the school is a furniture store. Will it be demolished too one day, or—I admit the idea amuses me—might it be sold and converted into a 'unique character residence'? Emma, for whom it had seemed a dream come true, did not long survive the inevitable leaving of the school house when George retired, at nearly seventy, from the caretaking job he had taken in desperation after the First World War. She had a massive stroke. As she lay immobile and speechless, nursed tenderly week after week, month after month, by the man whose prop she had been for over half a century, whose children she had borne and whose vicissitudes she had shared, what were *her* thoughts? Of all the people in Mary's story it is Emma, 'our Mother', whom I most regret I came too late to interview, and record. To the end a contradiction, impulsive and wise, passionate and authoritarian, sometimes unfair, often generous, a product of a world all but vanished, she compels and repels me: a matriarchal figure in a fading landscape.

Many of the working girls have gone too: Sis first, in her early forties, all but one of Mary's sisters, Kate who danced lightly as a bird. In 1973 Flowers Brewery was razed to the ground, and a piece of Stratford's history disappeared forever. As for Mary herself, if she still had dreams, like most of us she suppressed them. She never went back to 'mechanical work', although her factory days were not quite over, nor did she ever again see the one figure she had so hoped might be there one day, in the porch. She seldom spoke of him, and when she did it was with quiet scorn. She had her son. *He* had been the loser, in the last analysis.

And perhaps he would have agreed. Confounding all predictions of an early and violent death, as if by magic he appeared one day in 1984 on the other side of the world, in the heartland of cinematic fantasy: Los Angeles. My husband Brian and I went to see him. White haired, with laughing eyes and stories of his own to tell, he was still, for all his material assets, a man alone. He had done some admirable and some not so admirable things. 'I am,' he said ruefully, 'an asshole.' It was hard not to like him. He remembered a girl turning cartwheels on a pavement long ago in England, and when we said goodbye he wept.

Mary had dried her tears years before, and eventually in the fullness of time she married: a kind, unselfish man. Did she live happily after? Her expectations were modest. She loved a laugh and a chat, and from time to time she still got on other people's wedding photographs. Cheerfully she supplemented the family income with seasonal work on the farms, and cleaning jobs. She was a good wife, although her son remained the centre of her universe and she did not seem disappointed when there were no more children. Once, a shadow appeared on her lung, but went away and with it the last breath of another, more poignant ghost from her past. She lived in the present, and 'made do'. In short, she survived.

✻

When our Mother died, Cyril said: 'Take this, our Mary, get yourself a new coat.'

I thought, I'll buy a red *costume*. It ended up in a rug, that costume, in a great big centre circle of red. We was so *relieved*, you see, for her. It was over.

'Where'll *you* go?'

He thought of a place. 'Newcastle,' he said, 'I couldn't stick it 'ere.'

'*New*—castle?'

'Yes.'

'God 'elp our Dad.'

It was the first time we had ever said that.